Narrative R$_x$

A Quick Guide to Narrative Medicine for Students, Residents, and Attendings

Arthur Lazarus, MD, MBA

© 2025 University of California Health Humanities Press

University of California
Center for Health Humanities
Department of Humanities and Social Sciences
UCSF (Box 0850)
490 Illinois Street, Floor 7
San Francisco, CA 94143-0850

www.UCHealthHumanitiesPress.com

This series is made possible by the generous support of the Dean of the School of Medicine at UCSF, the UCSF Library, and a Multicampus Research Program Grant from the University of California Office of the President. Grant ID MR-15-328363 and Grant ID M23PR5992.

Designed by Virtuoso Press

Library of Congress Control Number: 2025934828

ISBN (pbk): 979-8-9926888-0-1
ISBN (hbk): 979-8-9926888-1-8
ISBN (ePub): 979-8-9926888-2-5

Printed in USA

ALSO BY ARTHUR LAZARUS

Neuroleptic Malignant Syndrome and Related Conditions (co-author)

Controversies in Managed Mental Health Care

Career Pathways in Psychiatry: Transition in Changing Times

MD/MBA: Physicians on the New Frontier of Medical Management

Every Story Counts: Exploring Contemporary Practice Through Narrative Medicine

Medicine on Fire: A Narrative Travelogue

Narrative Medicine: The Fifth Vital Sign

Narrative Medicine: Harnessing the Power of Storytelling through Essays

Story Treasures: Medical Essays and Insights in the Narrative Tradition

21st Century Schizoid Health Care: Essays and Reflections to Keep You Sane on Your Medical Travels

To those who seek meaning in medicine – may these stories inspire, sustain, and remind you of the healer within.

Contents

Preface viii

Introduction: Storykeepers – The Hidden Duty of Doctor x

Section 1: Writing and Reflection: Tools and Techniques

1. Opening Up 1
2. Bad Grammar Makes Me Mad. I Can't Help It 5
3. The Application of Creative Nonfiction to Medical Practice 9
4. Achieving Literary Competence in Medical Students 14
5. Incorporating Memoir in Narrative Medicine Writing 19
6. Exploring the Connection Between Creativity and Narrative Medicine Writing 22
7. Is Storytelling Hard-Wired into Our Brains? 25
8. Was Munchhausen the Ultimate Storyteller? 29
9. A Few Rules to Consider When Writing Narratives 32
10. The Enchantment of Writing and Telling Stories 36
11. Good Writers Borrow. Great Writers Steal! 39
12. Write What You Want to Know About, Not About What You Know 43
13. Writing in the "Shadow of the Text" 46
14. Our Secret Life Comes Out in Prose and Poetry 49
15. Daydreaming and the Default Mode Network in Narrative Creation 53
16. How Does the Writer's Mood Affect the Writing and Rewriting of Narratives and Memoir? 57
17. Shepherd Your Story – and Help Others Shepherd Their Own ... 60
18. Scams Perpetrated on Physician Authors by Impersonators and Bad Actors 64
19. Publish or Perish Your Way to Tent City 68
20. We Shouldn't Let Case Reports Become a Lost Art 72
21. The Importance of Plain Language in Writing and Medical Practice 76
22. Someone Called Me "Boswell." It was a Compliment of the Highest Order 80

23.	Writers: Beware of Lies, Damned Lies, and Statistics	8
24.	Overcoming Writer's Block	8
25.	Should You Publish Your Narrative?	9

Section 2: The Five-Minute Narrative: Insights for Today's and Tomorrow's Doctors

FOR MEDICAL STUDENTS

26.	Is It Noble or Selfish to Never Practice Medicine After Getting a Medical Degree?	9
27.	How Will Tomorrow's Medical Students be Different?	1
28.	What if Medical Students Were Taught the Way Musicians Learned How to Play?	1
29.	Is Your Medical Specialty Sustainable?	1

FOR RESIDENTS

30.	The Not-So-Private Lives of Young Physicians	1
31.	PTSD After Medical Education	1
32.	Reconsidering the Art of Medicine	1
33.	Why Not Do Your Residency Where You Went to Medical School?	1

FOR ATTENDINGS

34.	Avoid Burnout by Finding Your Fit in the Organization	1
35.	Leaving a Toxic Workplace – And Preparing for One Less Toxic	1
36.	Does Ageism Lurk Behind Mandatory Retirement?	1
37.	Are Physicians with MBAs Traitors to Health Care?	1
38.	Let's Not Discourage Our Children from Becoming Doctors	1

FOR EVERYONE

| 39. | Are Your Hobbies Connected to Your Specialty? | 1 |
| 40. | The Impact of Imposter Syndrome on Physicians' Practice and Leadership Development | 1 |

41.	Reflections on Human Suffering	160
42.	What are the Qualities of Exceptional Physicians?	164
43.	Practicing Medicine with Conviction	168
44.	AI Overtakes Humans – Fantasy or Reality?	173
45.	Political Discussions in the Doctor-Patient Relationship	178
46.	How Will You Make Your Mark on Medicine?	182
47.	The Dual Role of Illusion in Patient Care	186
48.	The Decline of Whole-Person Treatment in Modern Medicine	190
49.	The Secret to Improving Healthcare Services	195
50.	Disability Redefines "Ability" in the Medical Profession	199
	Afterword: The Graduation Speech I've Longed to Give	203
	Notes and Sources	208
	About the Author	209

Preface

In the demanding world of medical education and practice, time is our most precious commodity. For students, residents, and seasoned attendings alike, days are consumed by complex diagnoses, challenging cases, and the weighty responsibility of patient care. In the middle of this whirlwind, it can be difficult to remember why we chose this path in the first place and what we can gain – and give – through reflection, writing, and storytelling. This book is an invitation to return to the heart of medicine through the lens of narrative.

Narrative medicine is not merely writing vignettes that pay tribute to our patients; it's about listening deeply, understanding context, and fostering empathy. Though often perceived as an abstract add-on to the "real" work of clinical training, narrative medicine is, in fact, an essential skill. This book provides a bridge into the narrative world, designed to fit seamlessly into a busy schedule. It consists of 50 short, carefully crafted essays, each of which can be read in about five minutes. These essays, mostly culled from my previous works, delve into the essence of reflective writing, explore the power of story in medicine, and provide practical techniques for engaging in narrative custom, all without distracting from the rigorous demands of medical training and practice.

Throughout these pages, you'll encounter recollections and insights from my experiences with patients, colleagues, and years in clinical practice and management. The essay format has allowed me to tackle some of medicine's most pressing issues: the evolving healthcare system, the toll of physician burnout, the challenges of medical school and residency training, and the deeply personal ethical struggles that confront us all. The goal is to bring to light the value of self-reflection and shared stories, showing how they help us find meaning in our work, connect with patients, and support each other along the way.

For students, this book introduces narrative medicine as a tool to enrich your understanding of patients' experiences and your own development as a clinician. For residents, it serves as a reminder to pause and find moments of clarity amid intense schedules. And for attendings, these essays offer a renewed perspective on the significance of stories in sustaining a long and fulfilling career. In conceiving this book, my intent was to capture the hesitant scribbles of a medical student's first reflective piece, to let the pages carry the pulse of a patient's story told in a resident's weary but determined voice, and to transform a seasoned physician's crisp, annotated chart entries into a narrative that bridges human connection and clinical care.

As you navigate the rigors of medical training and practice, these quick-read commentaries offer a breather, a chance to consider the broader landscape of our profession. Why not carry Narrative Rx with you in the classroom, on clinical rotations, on rounds, and in the office? I designed it with that in mind, as a companion to treatment offering a quick dose of insight, empathy, or clarity just when you need it. Each essay is meant to serve as a brief respite, a minute to step back, reflect, and reconnect with the core values that drew you to medicine in the first place. Whether you're in a quiet corner between patients or winding down after a demanding shift, this book is here to remind you that your journey in medicine is as much about the stories you carry as the science you practice.

As you make your way through the narratives, may you find encouragement, inspiration, and connection to the deeper purpose of medicine. View each essay as a doorway to deliberation, a pause in the rush, and an opportunity to reconnect with the healer within. Let the stories remind you that every patient matters, and every voice needs to be heard. Let the reflections become a quiet guide on your path, illuminating the timeless bond between practice and narrative.

Introduction

Storykeepers – The Hidden Duty of Doctors

"We all die twice. Once when our bodies give out. And again, when our stories stop being told." This quote is attributed to the fictional character Dr. Donald "Ducky" Mallard, the NCIS forensic pathologist played by the late beloved actor David McCallum. However, nowhere in the Hippocratic Oath does it say physicians have a duty to propagate the memories of their patients. Quite the opposite, it instructs doctors to maintain their confidentiality. It is incumbent on us, as physicians, to break that bind – ethically, of course – and capture the essence of legacy, i.e., how our patients live on through the stories we share about them.

The role of "storykeeper" is practically unacknowledged in medical training but is vital to preserving the human side of healthcare. Stories sustain the memories of patients long after their physical presence is gone. The entire ethos of narrative medicine implores us to honor and cherish our patients' stories, ensuring they are not lost in the shuffle of medical charts and diagnoses.

When I ask physicians, "Why aren't you writing about your patients and clinical experiences?" the most common answer is: "I don't know how to get a story onto the page." One approach that has consistently worked for me is to examine the role of stories in healing, reflecting on how they sustain the memory of patients after they have passed on, whether in the literal sense or after they have left my practice. Narrative medicine, in particular, provides a framework for paying tribute to our patients and preserving their memories by preserving their stories, those told to us in the exam room, at the hospital bedside, before a procedure, and in other medical settings.

Writing about individuals whose stories are (or were) important to them may also have an impact on us, perhaps altering our lives, practice, or career. Paying it forward illustrates how patients' narratives can continue to resonate, shaping the ways we think about treatment and the doctor-patient relationship. Such reflections might naturally lead to a broader conversation about the importance of deep, active listening in the medical profession, as well as ways in which stories about doctors, themselves, might endure, influencing others through their words, actions, or teachings.

The dual role of narrative medicine as both a therapeutic tool and a means of immortality is compelling. By telling and retelling stories, we create a web of shared experiences that connects generations of patients and providers. This collective narrative preserves not only individual lives but also the kindness of compassionate care. These themes are deeply interconnected and offer countless possibilities for crafting a reflective, impactful narrative.

As a starting point for writing, I suggest you think about stories as a way of delineating a person's essence. From there, reflect on how physicians uniquely occupy a position of unmatched intimacy as witnesses to life-changing moments in patients' lives. This perspective grants doctors a singular ability – and responsibility – to act as custodians of their patients' stories. You will find that everyday medical encounters readily lend themselves to narrative writing and can bring depth to your composition. Personal anecdotes or vignettes will illustrate moments when telling a patient's story can make a lasting impact on others. Narrative medicine provides a natural framework for creative nonfiction, translating patient care into a story of empathy and understanding.

The main challenge, as I mentioned, is balancing respect for patient confidentiality with the need to share narratives that teach and inspire. A physician's oath to the profession, coupled with HIPAA regulations, can stymie good writing. As a psychiatrist, I have had to be extra careful about how much and what type of information to disclose, necessitating biographical, geographical, and other changes to the narrative to prevent identification of the patient, whether living or not. If you want to share a story about a patient, it's always best to obtain their permission or the permission of loved ones (if the patient is deceased) while also disguising or omitting elements that could reveal their identity.

Here is how a colleague handled this delicate situation. He wrote, "I wanted to honor a local teenager in my town who sadly took his life several years ago. I coached this kid in soccer and knew his family pretty well. Before I submitted my tribute for publication, I asked their permission and asked them to read it, fearing I might upset them. They thanked me for addressing the topic [of suicide] and for honoring their son. And they gave me a 'definite yes' when I asked their permission to submit it [for publication]."

The emotional weight of holding sad (or triumphant) stories can be enormous. Maya Angelou famously said: "There is no greater agony than bearing an untold story inside you," referencing her own experiences of trauma and silencing during her childhood in the segregated south, where she endured a traumatic sexual assault that left her speechless for a period of time. Sharing and preserving patient stories ensures that their lives – and your involvement in their care – will continue to reverberate, shaping the culture of medicine and the broader human experience. The ripple effect can extend well beyond any one individual encounter.

As a denouement to this essay, it is only fitting that I reveal the spark for writing it, to let you know stories can originate virtually anywhere and at any time. While I was watching an episode of NCIS ("The Stories We Leave Behind"), I was moved by the closing dialogue between "Jimmy" (Dr. Palmer, played by Brian Dietzen) and "Tony" (Michael Weatherly, in a reprise role) as they were preparing to attend "Ducky's" funeral.

Jimmy: "I'm really glad you're here, Tony."

Tony: "Wouldn't miss it [Ducky's funeral] for the world."

Jimmy: "Been telling stories all week about Dr. Mallard. You know. The whole team. A lot of stories. I guess that's...that's all we have in the end, right? Is just... just the stories we leave behind."

Tony: "Hmm. I wouldn't say only that, Jimbo. We also have the lives we touch while we are here. The people we leave behind."

My message to you is: Touch – and be touched by – your patients. Be their storykeeper. Keep your patients alive by sharing their stories. Put their stories

– and your stories – onto paper, as often as possible. Do not leave your patients behind. Sustain them in your narratives. Honor their lives and ensure that their voices, lessons, and journeys will continue to serve as a benefit and a blessing.

SECTION 1

Writing and Reflection:
Tools and Techniques

1.
Opening Up

"Writing holds the potential for comfort and insight to come from your difficult or painful experiences."
—John Fox, in *Poetic Medicine*

Of all the attributes ascribed to great writers and writing, perhaps being open and available to oneself is the most important because it allows for genuine self-reflection and authenticity, enabling writers to connect deeply with their readers through honest and relatable narratives. Opening up comes easy to me because I am a psychiatrist. I was "opened up" in psychotherapy, and I helped my patients "open up" in their therapy. Yet when it came time for me to write a brief passage about the process of "opening up," I struggled.

I had to put myself in the uncomfortable position of allowing myself to free associate, much like I would have done in psychoanalysis, never knowing where the narrative leads you. Opening up, like free associating, requires that we cast off "structure," allowing thoughts and emotions to flow freely and unfiltered. It doesn't sit well with medical trainees and practicing physicians because the medical field often emphasizes structured thinking, evidence-based approaches, and precision, which can make embracing unstructured, open-ended exploration feel awkward and counterintuitive.

I suggest you write a brief passage, maybe 800 to 1200 words, about what it means to "open up." Be honest with yourself. Don't try to hide your warts and blemishes. Expose your inner feelings and thoughts. I guarantee you are not alone. Paraphrasing Maya Angelou, we are more alike than unalike. Only when you become comfortable in your own skin will you realize the power of the written word.

What follows is a brief passage reflecting my attempt to "open up" for an assignment in writing class:

Here is what I know to be true: reading – close reading – and writing opens up a rewarding path for inquiry, reflection, understanding, and creativity that is ultimately healing.

The process of "opening up" is marvelous to watch, whether it's witnessed in psychotherapy or seen in nature. Flowers and plants, like people, come into bloom. New trees become part of the forest canopy. Even onions bloom!

Nature takes her time to "open up," and people do, too. People, like flowers, need time to emerge from their fragile bulbs and blossom. Once in bloom, they need to be nurtured.

Some people open up in tandem with nature: cyclical. After they open, they close for a period of time. They drop their petals and wither, only to blossom the following season. Perhaps they are perennials.

I've seen plants shut down due to insufficient nurturing, or a lack of rain or sunshine. Some plants are abused and neglected. Unlike perennials, whose regrowth is programmed, these plants do not open on cue. They are fragile. They need TLC.

Upon viewing wilted plants in my office, a patient said she could no longer see me. "If you can't take care of your plants," she sighed, "how do you expect to take care of me?"

Ultimately, nature, like people, are unpredictable. They are like large sections of forest that have been leveled by severe storms or landslides.

Traumatic events in nature have the power to radically change the forest's appearance.

Traumatized people are no different. They may or may not be capable of regaining their footing, of repairing themselves, of returning to baseline. Like the forest, their character may be damaged forever.

I "opened up" late in life. You could say I was a "late bloomer." I walked and talked late. I entered puberty late. I was socially stunted and intellectually blunted.

I blossomed in medical school, graduating AΩA, and later, number one in my executive MBA program.

The point is that people open up at different times and under different circumstances. Children's brains mature at different rates, and some – not all – will become emotionally intelligent as well as natively intelligent.

Parents fret about their children and worry excessively, hoping one day they'll bloom – or maybe not ever, infantilizing them.

"Opening up" is a term I first encountered in psychotherapy, as a psychiatric resident. My analyst told me I was anxious because I put myself in my patients' shoes, a sign that I was "open" to their needs, perhaps even afraid of "catching" their hallucinations.

Medical students have similar fears, but not to that extreme. Students have exaggerated worries about their health. Maybe they, too, need therapy.

Whether you are in therapy, or are becoming a therapist, the process of "opening up" can be remarkable, if handled correctly. My analyst leaned forward, crossed his index fingers, and held them close to my face. "Art, you can empathize with your patients and I guarantee you will not catch their conditions."

What a gallant attempt to open me up – and it worked, for a while. But other fears set in that made it difficult for me to continue practicing. I closed down.

I think my analyst was correct when he said the process of "opening up" can resemble a psychedelic trip. The lines between reality, wish, and fantasy can easily become blurred. Strong emotions may even produce psychotic-like thoughts.

One of my supervisors said that the closest thing to psychosis that normal people experience is falling in love. He called it "the rush." The experience is very primordial, and it only lasts six months, he told us.

I have fallen in love. I have been in therapy. I have conducted therapy. I have lived to prove others wrong. Now I am learning to write from my heart.

All these efforts involve "opening up." None have caused me to "hear voices" or "see things." I am still grounded. My reality testing is good. I am loved by my family, and they love me.

My writing is less formal. I have freedom to be creative. I am comfortable using plain language. I write in a more conversational tone. I have broken the academic chains. I have embraced storytelling in my writing.

I have opened up.

2.
Bad Grammar Makes Me Mad. I Can't Help It.

Ensuring your prose is grammatically correct and free of errors involves a combination of self-editing techniques, leveraging technology, and seeking feedback.

Some of the most brilliantly funny men have had the saddest personal lives. John Belushi, Chris Farley, and Sam Kinison were all preceded by Jerome Lester Horwitz, otherwise known as Curly of the Three Stooges: n'yuk-n'yuk-n'yuk. Why, soitenly the tragic life of a comedic legend deserves a great biography, and while Curly's niece (Moe's daughter) did her best to amass a wealth of Curly memorabilia – a mixture of written material and rare photographs of Curly's family, films, and personal life – the book was poorly written and edited, and it contained multiple spelling and grammar errors. The author proudly claimed she wrote the book in less than 90 days, and it shows.

If it makes your blood boil when you read prose punctuated incorrectly and containing bad grammar, you are not alone. A study from researchers at the University of Birmingham found that when certain people come across grammar errors, their bodies respond physically. Departures from linguistic normality (i.e., errors in grammar, syntax, and punctuation) trigger a clear cardiovascular reaction – decreased heart rate variability, which may signal several potential health issues – and the cardiovascular response becomes stronger as the writing violations become more frequent.

The researchers also discovered that the physiological responses were less severe when the study subjects had to deal with grammatical mistakes spoken by someone with a foreign accent (in this case, Polish). Listening to a foreign speaker didn't itself affect the subjects' heart rate. That suggests participants, who were British, expected a non-native speaker to make more grammatical mistakes and were more forgiving of those mistakes.

The study was conducted so that 41 healthy, British English-speaking adults listened to 40 English speech samples, half of which contained grammatical errors. The texts were read in a native British and a Polish accent by both a male and a female voice. Participants were instructed to listen to the four different speakers in both error-free and error-ridden conditions. Listening to speech containing errors reduced heart rate variability, and the reduction tended to be proportional to the number of mistakes.

The authors concluded: "The observation brings into focus a new dimension of the intricate relationship between physiology and cognition, suggesting that cognitive effort reverberates through the physiological system in more ways than previously thought." In other words, becoming upset at someone who uses bad grammar is reflexive. It's in our DNA. It can feel like an assault on our system.

No wonder misplaced apostrophes make me angry. I live near Charlotte, North Carolina, home to Bojangles, a restaurant chain founded in 1977 and known for its "chicken 'n biscuits," now served at over 800 locations in 15 states. Fans from all over know Bojangles for their catchy tagline – "It's Bo Time!" However, the company has been too chicken to even say where the apostrophe in its name is supposed to go. Is it Bojangle's or Bojangles' – or simply Bojangles without an apostrophe? Over time, the final apostrophe has migrated several times.

Actually, at one time, the official Bojangles logo included an apostrophe flat above the S – not before or after. "The only plausible explanation," according to The Grammarian, otherwise known as Jeffrey Barg, "is that the restaurant chain couldn't decide whether the apostrophe was supposed to go before or after the S, so it split the difference like splitting a perfectly flaky biscuit."

The restaurant was initially spelled "Bojangle's," like McDonald's. In its most recent incarnation, there is no apostrophe. The punctuation free logo is clearly at odds with rules for the use of possessive apostrophes (don't get me started on the 'n). To make matters worse, the "j" in Bojangles is dotted by a five-point star rather than a *tittle*, which is the name of the small distinguishing mark (the dot) that should appear over a lowercase *i* (and a lowercase *j*).

At least there is no confusing the restaurant with the song, "Mr. Bojangles," written by Jerry Jeff Walker, a 1970 hit for the Nitty Gritty Dirt Band and a favorite of Sammy Davis Jr.'s. But hold the gravy 'n biscuits. The restaurant's founders *did* name the establishment after the song. It came to them as they were driving along the highway and heard it, according to Jackie Woodward, formerly the chief marketing officer at Bojangles. Furthermore, in an interview with *The Washington Post*, Woodward confessed, "What makes my job so much fun is that people do care about whether Bojangles has an apostrophe or not. It shows the passion that our customers have for our food."

I don't pretend to be a culinary expert or an expert in linguistics, but obvious grammar mistakes rile me. They are visible to everyone, and egregious errors indicate a lack of fundamental knowledge and/or proofreading. That's why I am so grateful for professional editors – they've saved my hide countless times. One that I have worked closely with jokingly told me that she spends her time "placing missing commas." Another editor told me she could reduce my word count by "taking out slivers [of words], like a fine surgeon's scalpel," and I wouldn't notice anything was missing!

Apart from proofreading your work and consulting an editor, there are many ways to ensure your prose is grammatically correct and free of errors and mistakes, e.g., use automated online or software tools, read your work aloud, share it with a friend or writing group, read a physical copy as opposed to viewing it on a computer screen – and don't rush through it.

Despite his mispronunciations, Curly had an uncanny ability to instantly spell big words, such as "chrysanthemum," if asked. The gag was that he never did it when something important was at stake. But your writing is important. Don't become a victim of soikemstance by not asking for editorial help. Indubitably!

3.
The Application of Creative Nonfiction to Medical Practice

There are myriad ways doctors and patients have incorporated creative nonfiction into their daily routines.

When Oscar Wilde was asked how he spent his morning, he answered: *"I spent it revising a poem."*

"What changes did you make?"

"I took out a comma."

"What did you do in the afternoon?"

"I put it back."

Most writers have a preferred style of writing, using somewhat repetitive grammar, phrasing and syntax, choosing words that are familiar and seem reliable, ones that can be counted on to make their stories clear to readers. However, the best writing, in my opinion, shows the most variety; the writing is not predictable or redundant, and the writers are comfortable crossing genres. But just what are the main genres of narrative medicine writing?

First there is poetry. Many of us have a jaundiced view of poetry based on antiquated notions and negative impressions, most gleaned from our formative years. Modern poetry today is quite different, however, and quite accessible. I could not do justice to its beauty in a short paragraph or two. Suffice it to say that poetry is the least rule-oriented form of writing. Detailed knowledge about poetic forms is fascinating and helpful, but it's not required for writing poetry. Ironically, that may explain why some doctors struggle writing poetry – it contradicts all the ways they were raised and trained: by rules, and with structure. The only rule in writing poetry – indeed, creative writing in general – is that there are no rules (or very few). What works, works. That's the science of it! (However, I did come up with a few rules in essay 9.)

My narrative medicine instructor said that we change with every poem we write, and I do not think she was exaggerating. The Medici were fans of poetry and art for this reason. They saw it as a means to *renovatio* – to renew themselves and renovate humanity. My teacher then dispelled a myth. She said, "I know that so many conversations around poetry and writing are about 'revision.' Good writing is '10% inspiration and 90% perspiration.'" Then she exclaimed, "It's not true!" Her advice to our class, and mine to you, is to write and just keep writing and you'll find that each new poem will reflect a new aspect of yourself. I recommend John Fox's *Poetic Medicine* as a good companion reader if you want to learn more about the "how to" of writing poetry.

At the opposite end of the writing spectrum is fiction. Physicians are natural storytellers by virtue of their training, recounting patients' detailed histories since medical school. The medical profession is rife with outstanding physician storytellers including W. Somerset Maugham, Sir Arthur Conan Doyle, Oliver Wendell Holmes, and Anton Chekhov, along with more contemporary authors such as Robin Cook, Michael Crichton, and Walker Percy.

Percy, a Columbia-trained physician best known for his philosophical novels set in and around New Orleans, remarked, "I was the happiest man ever to contract tuberculosis, because it enabled me to get out of Bellevue [hospital] and quit medicine." Chekhov, a master of short stories, captured the appeal of writing fiction when he wrote: "Medicine is my lawful wife and literature my mistress; when I get tired of one, I spend the night with the other."

The fiction writer "Doug Zipes" – also known as Douglas P. Zipes, MD, Distinguished Professor Emeritus at Indiana University School of Medicine – is one of those physicians who has a mistress. He wrote: "I emphasized recently that life's journey is more important than the finish. This is particularly applicable to my late-blooming career in fiction ... Fiction allows for the creative freedom to invent your own universe, to imagine a world without boundaries, to conceive characters you love and make into heroes, or characters you hate that you can kill if you so choose. It is exhilarating and a world apart from writing tightly regulated science."

The sweet spot for me lies between poetry and fiction and is termed "creative nonfiction," and at other times "narrative nonfiction." Creative nonfiction appears to be an oxymoron, but the genre has deep literary roots. Lee Gutkind, author of *Keep It Real: Everything You Need to Know About Researching and Writing Creative Nonfiction*, is closely associated with this style of writing, "which presents or treats information using the tools of the fiction writer while maintaining allegiance to fact."

The creative nonfiction writing style tends to be dramatic and imaginative, but it never crosses the line into fiction because the content portrays a factually accurate account of real people and events, although in a compelling, vivid manner. "To put it another way," Gutkind explains, "creative nonfiction writers do not make things up; they make ideas and information that already exist more interesting and often more accessible ... Creative nonfiction writers have a complicated obligation to their readers: to entertain like novelists but to educate like journalists."

Narrative medicine writing is essentially creative nonfiction applied to medical practice. Narrative medicine employs techniques similar to creative nonfiction writing to tell stories and convey medical information. The application of creative nonfiction to medical practice can enhance the art of medicine and improve health outcomes. It can bridge the gap between science and humanity, and between physicians and patients. Creative nonfiction, like narrative medicine, can be applied in various other ways to enhance patient care, medical education, and research communication.

For example, creative nonfiction can be used to write patients' stories, which can help physicians better understand patients' experiences, perspectives, and emotions. This can lead to more empathetic care and improved patient satisfaction. It can also help patients better understand their own medical conditions and treatment plans. I wrote and published many case reports when I began my medical career (see essay 20). Although most of these reports leaned toward the rules of science and hence the writing style appeared rigid, creative liberties could be taken, for example, in describing the patient's personal, family and social history.

Creative nonfiction can be especially useful in medical education to teach students about the humanistic aspects of medicine. It can help students understand the psychological and social aspects of diseases and the impact of illnesses on patients' lives. This can lead to the development of more compassionate and holistic physicians. Writing programs have become wildly popular in medical schools, usually advertised under the banner of "narrative medicine," "creative writing," "reflective writing," and "creative nonfiction," attesting to the considerable overlap between these styles and categories.

Creative nonfiction can be used to communicate the results of medical research in a more accessible and engaging way. It can make complex medical information easier to understand and more relatable to a general audience. The best example is direct-to-consumer drug advertising, whether in print or on television. The results of clinical trials are presented to the audience in an impactful and memorable way, often with artistic and musical elements, yet the information conveyed must me accurate, truthful and not misleading.

Narrative medicine writing can serve as a form of reflection and self-care. It can help physicians process their experiences, cope with stress, and prevent burnout. A third of the students in my introductory class to narrative medicine were seasoned physicians. Some were on the verge of burnout or already there. But they eagerly looked forward to our weekly class sessions and were key participants.

Lastly, creative nonfiction can be used to convey public health messages in a more compelling way. It can help raise awareness about health issues and inspire people to take action. To give the public information on scientific issues that are complex and sometimes ethically contested, we must have writers who are skilled in presentation and have a thorough knowledge of medicine. Those who best fit that profile are doctors themselves.

4.
Achieving Literary Competence in Medical Students

Start reading. The choices are endless.

During college, I took two English courses: English composition (required), and world literature related to mental illness: a course aptly titled "Madness and Folly as Mirrors of Man Before the Age of Reason." With only these two courses, I was ahead of most of my medical school classmates in literary competence. It's a sad commentary on the weight given to the role of literature in preparation for medical school and a life thereafter.

Achieving literary competency in medical students aims to understand, appreciate, and use literature to enhance their professional development and improve patient care. It involves understanding that literature can provide valuable insights into the human experience of illness, health, and healthcare. Literature can provide medical students with a broader perspective on the human condition and the doctor-patient relationship.

In a classic study published in *Academic Medicine* in 1989, "Unmet Needs and Unused Skills: Physicians' Reflections on their Liberal Arts Education," physicians who graduated from three top-notch small liberal arts colleges between 1955 and 1982 were surveyed and said they wished they had taken more courses in the humanities – not only English literature, but also art, history and music – to better prepare them for dealing with practice and the vicissitudes of patient care. The greatest unmet need was reported to be "skill with people."

One of the conclusions reached by the study authors was that "the daily practice of medicine, in most cases, does not require immense scientific sophistication." Yet medical schools have scoffed at the idea of teaching humanities due to the constant growth of scientific and new medical advancements. Fortunately, progressive medical school admission committees now select more well-rounded college students, including applicants who have been exposed to literature and the humanities. Admission committees claim that exposure to literature can help develop a critical eye and research skills, as well as introduce students to ideas, cultures and views they may otherwise miss. Still, there are those who assert that the study of literature has goals and purposes unrelated to the medical profession, and that a strong science background should prevail.

I beg to disagree. Medical students need to be competent not only in the natural sciences but also in the social sciences and the humanities in order to converse intelligently with a heterogeneous health-conscious public. Literacy study can enrich medical students' moral education, foster a tolerance for the uncertainties of clinical practice, and provide a grounding for empathic attention to patients. Stories, essays, first-person narratives, and poetry also facilitate the professional identity formation of medical students. Ultimately, the development of medical professionalism will benefit from the critical and interrogative methods of literature.

It is not impossible for medical students to undertake a premedical curriculum that offers both scientific and literary competencies. The time to start reading is in high school, continuing (or catching up) in college, and devoting additional time to literature in medical school, residency and practice. Unless scholarly works from the humanities become part of the educational repertoire of physicians, they will fail to achieve the ideals embraced in the practice of medicine: namely, compassion, integrity, wisdom, and other virtues that are the foundation of the trust that is essential in the doctor-patient relationship.

Students whose professional identity has been guided by the study of literature should be able to:

- Consider multiple perspectives about what it means to be a doctor and a patient
- Think critically about the profession of medicine
- Comment insightfully about how the dyadic doctor-patient relationship is situated within larger societal dynamics and discourses
- Engage in reflective analysis of professional and ethical dilemmas
- Respond appropriately to various emotions that arise in themselves and their patients and families in response to diagnosis and treatment
- Develop a deep understanding of how culture shapes differences in communication

It is noteworthy that in the aforementioned study, a "willingness to be different" was reported as a prominent unused skill, suggesting that premedical students received a one-dimensional college education – mainly in the sciences – geared toward medical school acceptance. Physicians whose college educations fostered willingness to be different tended to choose less typical medical careers, potentially contributing to a more diverse physician workforce.

There are so many important works of literature that medical students may have missed out on while mastering the basic sciences. Here are some of my favorites, all written by physicians:

1. *The House of God* by Samuel Shem: This iconic novel provides a stark look at the realities of medical training, offering a critical perspective that encourages medical professionals to maintain compassion and empathy.

2. *Being Mortal: Medicine and What Matters in the End* by Atul Gawande: This book delves into the challenges of aging and death, discussing how medicine can not only improve life but also the process of its ending.

3. *The Man Who Mistook His Wife for a Hat* by Oliver Sacks: This collection of case histories of neurological disorders offers a compassionate and insightful look into the human mind and spirit. (*Seeing Voices: A Journey into the World of the Deaf*, also by Sacks, is a good alternative.)

4. *When Breath Becomes Air* by Paul Kalanithi: Written by a neurosurgeon diagnosed with stage IV lung cancer, this posthumously published memoir explores the nature of life and death, doctor and patient, and the relationship between health and identity.

5. *The Emperor of All Maladies: A Biography of Cancer* by Siddhartha Mukherjee: This Pulitzer Prize-winning book provides a comprehensive history of cancer, its treatments, and the ongoing search for a cure.

6. *What Doctors Feel: How Emotions Affect the Practice of Medicine* by Danielle Ofri. This book uses the author's rich personal and clinical vignettes to dissect the hidden emotional responses of physicians and show how these directly influence patients and treatment.

7. *My Own Country: A Doctor's Story of a Town and Its People in the Age of Aids* by Abraham Verghese. A heart-rending and evocative account of the early days of the AIDS epidemic, with tales of human suffering and endurance, and how a physician came to love a corner of Appalachia. (Anything written by Verghese is a good alternative.)

8. *In Shock: My Journey from Death to Recovery and the Redemptive Power of Hope* by Rana Awdish. By surviving a catastrophic medical event during pregnancy and countless complications, a critical care specialist is able to showcase the tremendous power of hope in the healing process.

These and many other works of literature can provide medical students with valuable insights into the human aspects of medicine beyond what they learn through science courses, textbooks, and clinical rotations. Stories impart communication skills and a sensitive appreciation of the multiple dimensions of practice. Above all, reading stimulates the development of students' personal values and an enduring sense of wonder at embodied human nature.

5.
Incorporating Memoir in Narrative Medicine Writing

"Memoir is the intersection of narration and reflection, of storytelling and essay writing."

— Patricia Hampl, in *Memory and Imagination*

"This isn't a memoir, is it?" You're not asking me to publish your memoir, are you?" This was the reaction I received from an editor when pitching my first collection of essays, *Every Story Counts*.

"Well, no, it definitely is not my memoir," I replied, "but yes, it does contain personal viewpoints and stories."

The word "memoir" originates from the French word "mémoire," which means "memory" or "reminiscence." The French term itself is derived from the Latin word "memoria," which also means "memory."

In English, the term "memoir" has been used since the 16th century to describe an individual's written account of their personal experiences and significant events in their life. It's a subset of the autobiographical genre, but it differs from an autobiography in that it usually focuses on a specific period or events in the author's life, rather than their entire life chronologically.

I think the harsh reaction I received from the editor was based on her thinking that memoir and autobiography are the same – they're clearly not. I was proposing a book of essays – much like this one – some containing memoir. (The word "essay" comes from the French word "essai," meaning "trial" or "attempt.")

Memoirs and personal essay collections are quite popular. Memoir writing – despite what William Grimes said in a critique for the *New York Times* (March 25, 2005), "We All Have a Life. Must We All Write About It?" – is not necessarily a bad thing. There are many wonderful, human, funny, and true stories out there. Individual stories, told well, have the power to change the world.

In *Keep It Real*, Lee Gutkind observes: "Memoir writing is not about self-obsession, even though the subject is invariably the experience of one life. Good memoirs should do what all good art aspires to do. They show us ourselves. This is arguably the distinction between good and bad memoir writing. Bad memoirs often offer readers the book equivalent of reality TV."

I wasn't asking the editor to publish my life's version of "Love After Lockup" or "The Real Housewives of…" And I certainly was not suggesting anything as salacious as "Naked and Afraid." The point is that bad memoir writing, like bad television, is self-indulgent and involves excessive contemplation of oneself or a single issue at the expense of a wider view and audience.

Gutkind continues, "A good memoir offers readers a human connection. A good memoir writer uses life experience, not to go more deeply into the self but to reach out to others. A good memoirist makes connections. A good memoirist's primary goal is to show us something true about ourselves, about what it means to be human … Individual human experience is valuable – in writing and elsewhere – only when it moves through, then transcends the self and connects to what's human in us all."

Gutkind's message is what was on my mind when I pitched my book to the editor. Fortunately, an editor working for a different publisher was on my wavelength, although she also balked until I sent her a dozen essays and an outline of the book. I understood her hesitancy, not only because there are bad memoirs, but also because incorporating memoir in narrative medicine writing can be a real turn off unless it has universal appeal. And the truth is, physician writers of medical memoir can be just as guilty of self-absorption as other kinds of writers of memoir. However, medical memoir can also be an important tool for forging connections and healing bonds among doctors and patients. Physician memoirs can offer inspiring accounts of life in medicine and medicine in life.

6.
Exploring the Connection Between Creativity and Narrative Medicine Writing

Dear Vincent,

    I hope this message finds you in good health despite your recent self-inflicted injury. The purpose of this letter is to discuss the intriguing relationship between creativity and narrative medicine writing. You told me you were certain such a link existed because you have witnessed a similar relationship among painters like yourself.

    Let me digress a moment for the sake of our readers.

    Narrative medicine writing is a form of writing that tells a factual story – usually about a patient – creatively, in a structured manner. Presumably there is a significant link between creativity and narrative medicine writing as there is in the realm of literature in general. Creativity fuels narrative writing by providing unique ideas and perspectives. It allows the writer to think outside of the box and to create a compelling, engaging narrative that captures the reader's attention.

    Creativity can manifest in medical narratives in various forms. For instance, it can bring a complex, multi-dimensional patient to life or describe unexpected events in the patient's history inventively and artistically. It can also be reflected in the way the writer uses language to convey emotions, set the scene, or describe physicians, caregivers and family members central to the narrative.

    Moreover, creativity in narrative medicine writing can enhance the reader's experience by making the narrative more vivid and engaging. It can lead to a deeper understanding and appreciation of the narrative by providing new insights and perspectives.

So, Vincent, now you know that creativity does, in fact, play a crucial role in narrative medicine writing, just as it does in painting and countless other mediums of self-expression. Creativity fuels engaging, thought-provoking narratives and enhances the reader's experience. Hence, nurturing creativity is essential for anyone involved in narrative writing.

How does one nurture creativity, you ask? You're under the impression that creativity is a trait we are born with – either we have it or we don't? And isn't there a connection between creativity and mental illness? You deem yourself expert on this topic, do you not, Vincent?

I can't give you definitive answers to all of those questions. Scholars have researched and written books about creativity, yet many points of contention remain. What I can say is that creativity can be practiced and learned to a degree. Everyone's creative process is unique, and each of us employs a combination of elements – some learned and others probably innate – to express what we want to write. Narrative writers also have tools that they learn how to apply to express their thoughts on paper.

For many writers – myself included – the element of surprise sparks creativity. Surprise rolls in like a tidal wave, totally unpredictable, when, like you, I am filling in my canvass yet not really knowing what should come next. Suddenly I surprise myself with a thought or a memory that, like a spark, catches fire and leads to something novel and creative. This moment of surprising myself as I write – or as you paint, I suspect – provides guidance: it reminds us where we have been and leads us to where we are going.

For example – and please forgive me Vincent for making this confession – I didn't originally intend to write to you. I began this letter with "Dear Reader" instead of "Dear Vincent," intending it for a general audience. I changed the salutation when I suddenly thought of you as I paused to reflect on creativity as it applies not only to writers but also to artists. How could I not think of you at such a time given that your mind is the embodiment of creativity, albeit driven toward unpredictable and self-destructive impulses.

I've read many accounts about your maladies, Vincent, and your doctors have given you a host of psychiatric diagnoses, most of them tainted by your excessive consumption of absinthe. Whatever mental affliction you may suffer, your moodiness seems to contribute to both your brilliance and baffling disorganization, which is evident in your paintings.

Perhaps you will find comfort in knowing that researchers have found connections between mood disorders – specifically bipolar disorder – and creativity: bipolar traits have been associated with enhanced creative expression in various occupations. Conversely, creativity plays a role in psychiatric treatment. Studies have shown that music and art therapy can be helpful for patients with schizophrenia, depression, and other mental disorders.

In summary, Vincent, I will say that narrative medicine writers tap into their creativity to reflect on their experiences as healers and the healed. They recognize that creativity is the process that blends medicine with the art and humanities. Their output is, ultimately, a story that can be shared with communities they care for. The question as to whether a connection exists between creativity and narrative medicine writing is perhaps best examined further by delving into its corollary: is storytelling hard-wired into our brains?

I'll follow up on that line of thinking in the next essay. That's all for now.

With warm regards,

Art Lazarus

7.
Is Storytelling Hard-Wired into Our Brains?

"Hey, did you hear the one about…?"
"How about a good bedtime story…?"
"You're not gonna believe this, but…"
"Can you tell me…"

Why, throughout human history, have people been so drawn to stories? Could it be because stories are first and foremost a survival mechanism? From an evolutionary standpoint, storytelling was a way to pass down vital information to ensure survival. Our ancestors shared stories to warn each other about dangers, share successful hunting strategies, or explain the world around them. This instinct to share and receive information through stories still drives our behavior – and it is indeed hard-wired into our brains.

In *The Sacred Balance: Rediscovering Our Place in Nature*, David Suzuki notes that our knack for narrative enables our ancestors to recognize, understand, and remember the meaning of patterns in nature, such as the migration of animals, the sequencing of the seasons, and the duration of night and day. In essence, the mind is telling itself a story aided by neural pathways constantly rewiring themselves to order sensory input.

Our stories, when jotted down on paper, become narratives. Our brains are programmed to learn and understand better through narratives. Telling stories and reading narratives activates many parts of the brains, sometimes for days. Whether you want your narrative to motivate, persuade or simply entertain, start with a story of human struggle – which is perfect for health narratives – and end it triumphantly. It will capture your readers hearts – by first attracting their brains.

Stories provide a structure that our minds easily comprehend and remember. They allow us to make sense of complex information by placing it in a context we can understand. One estimate suggests that we can recall facts up to 22 times more effectively when they are part of a story rather than just isolated data. So, if you want a fact to stick, the best thing to do is explain it with a story.

"The Epic of Gilgamesh" is perhaps the oldest written story on earth – a poem, actually, of adventure-filled tales. It is based on the real historical King of Uruk, Gilgamesh, who reigned around 2700 BC. The text we know today was written approximately 2100 BC and discovered on 12 clay tablets in cuneiform script in the mid-19th century. The fragments of the tablets were unearthed by archeologists in excavations across what is now Syria and Iraq, and they were painstakingly restored. The young man who decoded the tablets' puzzle was an English archaeologist named George Smith working for the British Museum.

Despite the date and place of its origin, the exploits of *Gilgamesh* showcase many of the same elements and themes still present in the stories enjoyed today by modern readers – a hero embarks on a difficult journey in which there is romance and seduction, encounters with strange and exotic characters, and impossible obstacles to overcome. Along the way, Gilgamesh rubs elbows with the gods and searches for the key to immortality – all with predictably tragic results. In a refrain that remains true today, the narrator remarks that no one truly dies as long as they are remembered by the living.

It is not a coincidence that the epic's themes of friendship, the fear of death, the pursuit of knowledge, and the search for immortality bear similarities to contemporary stories. Time does not seem to matter much to themes; nor indeed does location. A 2006 analysis of 90 folktale collections from around the world (from both tribal societies and industrialized ones) reveals as much, with scholars describing the presence of a number of distinctly common narratives covering basic human needs and desires in the stories they examined.

In *The Seven Basic Plots: Why We Tell Stories*, the late journalist and author Christopher Booker reasoned there are just seven of these universal plots, and they can be seen time and again in books, television shows, movies and even podcasts. They are:

1. Overcoming the Monster - *The War of the Worlds, Star Wars, Jaws*
2. Rags to Riches - *Cinderella, Jane Eyre, The Prince and the Pauper*
3. The Quest - *The Iliad, The Lord of the Rings, Raiders of the Lost Ark*
4. Voyage and Return – *Alice's Adventures in Wonderland, The Time Machine, Gulliver's Travels*
5. Comedy - *A Midsummer Night's Dream, Four Weddings and a Funeral, The Big Lebowski*
6. Tragedy - *Hamlet, The Great Gatsby, Citizen Kane*
7. Rebirth – *Groundhog Day, A Christmas Carol, The Shawshank Redemption*

Almost all stories can be simplified into one of these core themes. All categories engage our primal emotions and trigger and stimulate the release of neurochemicals like cortisol, dopamine, endorphins, and especially oxytocin, referred to as the "bonding hormone" or "love hormone." Compelling narratives cause oxytocin release and have the power to affect our attitudes, beliefs and behaviors. Oxytocin is also released in high amounts during childbirth and is believed to enhance empathy and emotional connections. This emotional engagement makes stories more memorable and impactful.

Simply telling stories can increase our empathy towards others we may have initially viewed as outsiders. That's why stories are a fundamental part of our social interactions and why storytelling has been an important tool for social cohesion for millennia: they allow us to share our experiences, understand others' perspectives, and foster connections. It's no surprise that social gatherings often revolve around the sharing of stories. In fact, it's estimated that as much as 65% of all human interactions take the form of social storytelling (i.e., gossip).

Stories stimulate our imagination and creativity. They allow us to explore different scenarios, solve problems, and think creatively, all of which are necessary for narrative writers. With around a hundred billion neurons and almost a quadrillion connections between the neurons in our brains, the organ borders on the wondrous, just like our stories. Yet, for all its complexity, the brain is still a pattern-seeking instrument that looks to put the chaos of the world into some kind of recognizable order.

Perhaps that is what the beloved Sufi scholar and poet Jalaluddin Rūmī understood when he wrote, "What you seek is seeking you."

8.
Was Munchausen the Ultimate Storyteller?

"The lies that people tell in stories is what makes them so true."
— Majid Kazmi

"The Epic of Gilgamesh" may be one of the earliest works of literature in the world, but surely the greatest storyteller of all time was Baron Hieronymus Karl Friedrich von Münchhausen (1720-1797), a German calvary officer.

The stories told by Baron Munchausen were fantastic and absurd, often featuring impossible achievements. They are a classic example of tall tales and the tradition of hyperbolic storytelling. Here are a few examples:

1. On a hunting trip, the Baron claims to have ridden on a cannonball, flown to the moon, and been swallowed by a giant fish, from which he escaped by tickling it with a feather.

2. In another tale, he pulls himself (and his horse) out of a swamp by his own hair.

3. In yet another story, he tells of a time when he was traveling in winter, and his horse was frozen in place overnight. When it was cut free, the horse was accidentally severed in half, and the half with the head and front legs ran off, only to return in spring perfectly healthy and whole.

The tales of Baron Munchausen have become a part of popular culture, referenced in a variety of media and spawning the term "Munchausen" to characterize pathological liars. Munchausen syndrome is familiar to doctors because it describes a psychiatric disorder in which someone pretends to be ill or deliberately produces symptoms of illness in themselves or others ("Munchausen by proxy"). Munchausen patients are bent on deceiving physicians by their conscious production of signs and symptoms of physical illness – and for no apparent gain other than to assume the role of a patient.

One of the characteristic features of Munchausen's syndrome is a tendency for patients to give a false but plausible history and seek out caregivers by wandering from hospital to hospital. They often demand hospitalization and request invasive diagnostic procedures and sometimes surgery. These patients are generally not suicidal or have a death wish, but a few have died in surgery.

I was consulted on several cases of patients suspected of having Munchausen's syndrome. I say "suspected" because the syndrome is nearly impossible to prove unless patients are caught in the act of fabricating their illness – for example, by pricking their finger and squeezing a few drops of blood into their urine specimen to simulate hematuria. When confronted with their surreptitious behavior, Munchausen patients typically deny it and move on, leaving the hospital against medical advice but to the delight of the housestaff.

Munchausen's syndrome was so-named by the British endocrinologist Richard Asher in 1951. Asher observed: "Like the famous Baron von Munchausen, the persons affected have always traveled widely; and their stories, like those attributed to him, are both dramatic and untruthful." The term "Munchausen's syndrome" is probably a misnomer, however, since the Baron himself was never chronically ill nor did he feign illness.

Asher considered Munchausen's syndrome to be similar to the Walter Mitty syndrome, in reference to the popular short story, "The Secret Life of Walter Mitty," in which the protagonist is engaged in never-ending reverie (see essay 14).

Unraveling the Munchausen legend has proven as challenging as the patients themselves. Apparently, the author of the Munchausen stories was not Munchausen himself but instead Rudolf Erich Raspe (1737-1794), also of dubious character. Accused of embezzlement, Raspe fled Europe disguised as a Dutchman and settled in London. Raspe anonymously published *Baron Munchausen's Narrative of His Marvelous Travels and Campaigns in Russia* in 1785. The book initially sold poorly, but after another publisher assumed responsibility for the printing, many volumes followed in rapid succession, all expanding on the original version.

Raspe's biographer, John Carswell, believed the Munchausen stories were actually an exaggeration of Raspe's own life, a projection of his "frustrated egotism." Raspe may have known Munchausen, since they were both from the same area of Germany. Munchausen died three years after Raspe, a humiliated and bitter man despite having achieved celebrity status. Munchausen never discovered the identity of the man who brought him unwelcome fame, that is, Raspe, whose antisocial behavior and fugitive existence was a facsimile of the typical Munchausen patient.

This tale is for real!

9.
A Few Rules to Consider When Writing Narratives

Rule #1: You rule!

Although I rarely eat at Outback Steakhouse, I've admired the Australian-themed restaurant chain's longstanding motto: "No Rules." Deep down, I dislike rules. A psychologist told me he could tell I was "anti-authoritarian" – without formally testing me. A psychiatrist described me as "irreverent." They were both correct. Essentially, I do not follow the rules (just ask my wife!).

The fact that there are very few writing rules in narrative medicine is one of the features that attracts me to it. But that doesn't mean you can write willy-nilly. What you put on paper begins with an understanding of the context of the narrative, and it must encompass several other attributes.

The **context** of a narrative is more than just background information. It is a vital part of understanding and treating the patient effectively. Clearly, the context of a narrative is crucial because it sets the stage for understanding the story, event, or situation being described. In a clinical setting, the context may include patient history, current symptoms, recent changes, and environmental factors. It provides necessary information that helps physicians and other healthcare providers interpret the patient's condition accurately. Setting the proper context for your narrative is key to making it impactful.

Authentic dialog, i.e., dialogue used to reveal character traits and advance the story, is equally important. The characters are real people, usually patients, and they should be portrayed with depth and complexity.

This includes showing their motivations, conflicts, growth, and changes over time. The dialog must therefore be authentic and reflective of the character's personality, background, and time period.

Truth and accuracy are paramount in medical narratives. The events, characters, dialogues, and settings must be as accurate as possible. Narrative medicine is a form of creative nonfiction. That means your narratives can (and should) be creative, but they can't take liberties with the truth. Often the "truth" must be reconstructed from memory, which could introduce historical distortion into the narrative. That's understood and considered okay in the world of narrative medicine, especially memoir, as long as the accounts actually occurred and are retold to the best of your ability.

While maintaining factual accuracy, writers can use **literary devices** such as foreshadowing, flashback, symbolism, metaphor, and simile to enhance the narrative. These literary devices can help physicians gain a deeper understanding of a patient's perspective. They can also make the narrative more engaging and memorable, thus improving communication and empathy between healthcare providers and patients.

Show, don't tell, is probably the closest thing to a commandment as there is in narrative medicine writing. You should aim to create vivid imagery and provoke emotion through detailed descriptions and accounts, rather than simply stating facts. Some authors suggest that you should show *and* tell. You are creating a work of art, not writing a patient's progress note or legal document. As I wrote in the Preface, in conceiving this book, my intent was to "show and tell."

Your narrative can be **structured** in various ways; it doesn't have to follow a linear timeline. However, the structure should serve the story and make it engaging for the reader. Because writing narratives often involves your reflection on the events – thoughts, feelings, and learning from the experience – a well-structured narrative allows for more effective **reflection**, as it provides a clear, organized account of the patient's experiences. Structure and reflection are two critical components that work together: structure provides the necessary framework for the narrative, while reflection allows for the extraction of meaningful insights from the story, leading to a more empathetic and comprehensive understanding of the patient's condition and experience.

Since narrative medicine is based on real events and people, thorough **background research** is essential. This can include interviews, reading documents or reports, visiting locations, etc. Good old-fashioned literature reviews are not out of the question, either. PubMed, a free web-based interface for searching MEDLINE, has been essential in my quest for scholarly knowledge that I integrate into narratives. PubMed has information about journal articles (approximately 25 million) published in 5,600 journals in 30 languages dating back to 1946. I probably spend as much or more time researching a topic as I do writing about it.

I caution you about using **artificial intelligence** (AI) in your research. ChatGPT and other large language models are known to occasionally be inaccurate and even "hallucinate" – manufacture or fabricate information: literature references, dates, and quotes. So, even if you use AI, you are obligated to verify the information as you would any other third-party content manager, e.g., websites. The use of AI to assist with grammar and writing may be helpful, but use it sparingly. Over-relying on AI can dilute your authenticity, hinder your personal growth, and compromise your unique voice that makes writing impactful.

You should respect the **privacy and dignity** of the people you write about. This might involve changing names or identifying details, particularly in sensitive situations. Asking patients and families for permission to share their stories is never a bad idea. Maintaining compliance with HIPAA is always a must. The physician and poet William Carlos Williams (1883-1963) wrote: "Their story, yours, mine – it's what we carry with us on this trip we take, and we owe it to each other to **respect our stories** (bold font added) and learn from them."

As with all writing, **revision** is key in narrative medicine. This involves reviewing your work for clarity, coherence, grammar, punctuation, and overall flow (refer to essay 2). Don't become overly obsessive, but check your work a few times before you consider it final. And don't get hung up on precise phraseology. Recreations of the past can change (see "truth" above). Be satisfied with your completed narrative, recognizing that it has inherent limitations owing to its inevitable subjectivity and point of view. There are many ways to say the same thing and convey the same meaning, and next time you may choose to do it differently.

Remember, while these are general rules, narrative medicine is a flexible genre and allows for considerable experimentation. Ultimately, there is only one rule to follow: You tell me your story; I'll tell you mine.

10.
The Enchantment of Writing and Telling Stories

Storytelling and writing can be pathways to enchantment, providing rich opportunities for discovering joy and meaning in work and life.

Writing is often viewed as judgment and anxiety producing, but eventually we learn how to get comfortable with the process. We settle down, and like meditation, writing becomes calming, even transformative, as we achieve a deeper, trance-like state where we become so wholly absorbed in what we're doing that we lose ourselves in the process. Quoting Diane Ackerman, the author of *Deep Play*, "We see the world in a richer way – more familiar than we thought, and stranger than we knew, a world laced with wonder." However, Ackerman continues, "Sometimes we need to be taught how and where to seek wonder."

There are many ways we can discover the wonders of writing and storytelling. Here is what stimulates and stokes me:

1. **Clinical Experience**: Medical professionals often encounter unique cases, new treatments, or interesting patient stories in their daily work. These experiences can provide a wealth of topics for medical narratives. My clinical encounters with patients have been the nucleus of my writing.

2. **Medical Research**: New research findings, advancements in medical technology, or controversial studies can all provide interesting topics for medical narratives.

3. **Current Events**: Health-related news stories, public health crises, or new healthcare legislation can be great sources of inspiration for medical

narratives.

4. **Patient Stories**: Patients' experiences and testimonials can provide a human-interest angle to medical narratives. These can range from stories of recovery and resilience to discussions about the challenges of living with a particular condition.

5. **Medical Conferences and Seminars**: These events often discuss the latest developments and trends in healthcare, which can provide new topics for medical narratives.

6. **Medical Journals**: Medical journals often contain case studies, research articles, and editorial pieces that can provide ideas for medical narratives. *JAMA*'s feature, "A Piece of My Mind," often motivates me to write.

7. **Professional Interactions**: Conversations with colleagues, mentors, or other healthcare professionals can spark ideas for medical narratives.

8. **Social Media and Online Forums**: These platforms provide newsfeeds, blogs, and insights into what patients and the general public are interested in or concerned about regarding healthcare, which can inspire relevant medical narratives.

9. **Personal Interests**: If the writer has a personal interest or passion within the field of medicine, this can often lead to engaging and insightful medical narratives.

10. **Feedback from Readers**: Comments and questions from readers can also provide ideas for new topics to explore in medical narratives. Many of my narratives were inspired by readers' reactions to online posts, including my own posts.

Deep Play suggests that the wonderment derived from writing can result in a state of enchantment – a transcendent experience where we feel a deep connection with the world around us. Ackerman emphasizes that these moments of enchantment can give us an incredible sense of joy, fulfillment, and meaning. Furthermore, she argues that in our fast-paced, technology-driven world, it's more important than ever to seek out these moments of enchantment to remind us of the beauty and wonder of existence.

Storytelling and writing are but one of many pathways to enchantment. They allow us to explore different perspectives, realities, and experiences, sparking our imagination and evoking a sense of wonder and fascination. They can transport us to different times and places, introduce us to new ideas and characters, and make us ponder deep questions about life, humanity, and the universe.

Perhaps that is why H.G. Wells' *The Time Machine* is one of my favorite books (and movies). It literally transports readers to different time periods, and the movie versions – 1960 and 2002 – excite wonder by asking which three books one would take to the future, realizing that the time traveler has removed three from his library (only the movie, not the novel, asks this question). The "three books" question sparks wonderment by inviting us to imagine which knowledge, stories, or values are so vital that they must endure into the future, evoking curiosity about the kind of world we might build with such choices (see also *Fahrenheit 451*/essay 17).

Additionally, the process of writing itself can be enchanting. Crafting a narrative, playing with language, and expressing our thoughts and emotions on paper can be deeply satisfying and fulfilling. It requires a heightened level of attention and focus, and in those moments of intense concentration, we may experience a sense of transcendence and joy.

Through storytelling, we not only enchant our lives but also those of the listeners, creating a shared human experience that is rich with emotion, learning, and connection. Writing is a calling to embrace enchantment as a path to a richer, more meaningful life, a state of "deep play" where we lose ourselves in the act and experience a tremendous connection with our inner world and the world around us.

11.
Good Writers Borrow. Great Writers Steal!

Abby Hoffman wrote Steal This Book. *Please don't do it!*

The phrase, "good writers borrow, great writers steal," is attributed to various writers including T. S. Eliot and Oscar Wilde. In *The Sacred Wood*, T. S. Eliot wrote: "Immature poets imitate; mature poets steal; bad poets deface what they take, and good poets make it into something better, or at least something different."

The idea behind the phrase "good writers borrow, great writers steal" and similar proclamations such as "talent borrows, genius steals," is that great artists don't merely imitate others; they take inspiration and ideas from various sources and transform them into something uniquely their own. It speaks to the creative process and the idea that innovation often involves building upon what has come before. The fact that this phrase is attributed to several different people proves how true the saying is.

William Shakespeare is often cited as a master of "stealing" ideas. Many of his plots were borrowed from earlier works or historical events, but he transformed them with his unique language, characterizations, and themes. For example, "Hamlet" draws heavily from earlier Scandinavian sagas and the works of Thomas Kyd, yet Shakespeare's treatment of the material is unparalleled.

Examples of "stealing" can also be found in endeavors other than literature. For example, The Beatles incorporated elements from various musical styles and artists into their own songs. "Come Together" was inspired by Chuck Berry's 1956 single "You Can't Catch Me," only slightly altering Berry's original lyric of "Here come a flattop / He was movin' up with me" to "Here come ol' flattop / He come groovin' up slowly."

In 2008, jazz piano legend Keith Jarrett filed a lawsuit against Steely Dan's Donald Fagen and Warner Bros. Music for copyright infringement. The lawsuit alleged that Steely Dan's song "Gaucho" contained unauthorized instrumental similarities to Jarrett's composition "Long As You Know You're Living Yours" from his 1974 album "Belonging." The case was settled in 2009 with the stipulation that Jarrett be included as a co-author of the track. In an interview after Gaucho was released, Fagen said that he loved the Jarrett track and had been strongly influenced by it.

Pablo Picasso's famous painting "Les Demoiselles d'Avignon" is said to have been influenced by African tribal masks and Iberian sculpture. Picasso took these influences and merged them with his own style, resulting in a groundbreaking work that paved the way for the Cubist movement.

Steve Jobs famously said, "Good artists copy, great artists steal" in the context of design and innovation at Apple. The original Macintosh, for example, borrowed ideas from Xerox PARC's graphical user interface but transformed them into a commercially successful product with its own unique features and design.

In each of these examples, the artists didn't merely replicate or mimic existing works; they took inspiration from them and reinterpreted them in a way that reflected their own creativity and vision. *New York Times* and bestselling author Ralph Pezzullo stated: "To my mind, it's not a question of borrowing or stealing; it's responding to the writing that turns you on, trying to imitate it, finding that imitation lacking, and in the process of striving to improve on it, stumbling upon a style of your own."

Author Ruth Culham admits to being a writing thief – and she encourages her students to become writing thieves, too! Her book, *The Writing Thief*, demonstrates a major part of good writing instruction is finding the right mentor texts to teach the craft of wiring. The book contains nearly 100 mentor texts along with activities aimed at teaching the traits of writing across the informational, narrative, and argument (opinion) modes. The use of mentor texts – carefully selected writing passages to illustrate specific elements of craft, style, structure, or genre – is a powerful teaching strategy that writers can learn from and apply to their own work.

The foregoing does not imply that because nothing is original you should steal from anywhere. Plagiarism is 100% wrong and guaranteed to end a writer's career – or any career that is heavily dependent on writing (academicians know this all too well). The key difference between stealing ideas in the creative sense and plagiarism lies in the acknowledgment and transformation of the source material.

When artists "steal" ideas, they typically acknowledge the influence or inspiration from the original source. They may not copy the work verbatim but instead use it as a springboard for their own creative expression. This acknowledgment can take various forms, such as citing the original source, referencing it in interviews or statements, or simply being transparent about the influence.

Great artists transform the borrowed ideas into something new and original. They don't merely replicate or reproduce the source material but reinterpret it through their unique perspective, style, or medium. This transformation involves adding their own creative elements, insights, or innovations, resulting in a work that stands on its own merits.

Plagiarism, on the other hand, involves passing off someone else's work or ideas as one's own without proper attribution or permission. It typically involves directly copying or closely imitating the original work without adding significant originality or value. Plagiarism is considered unethical and dishonest in creative and academic fields because it undermines the integrity of intellectual property and misrepresents the creator's contributions.

In the end, great writers will continue to take from the past and add to it, creatively turning their work into something different and perhaps deeper. Everyone borrows when creating a new work – no one is entirely original. However, what we do when we borrow, and our source of information or inspiration, matters. Art comes not from developing something completely different but from using the materials of the past to make something unique in the present which speaks to the future.

12.
Write What You Want to Know About, Not About What You Know

Ask the right questions, then "Make it so!"

If necessity is the mother of invention, then questions are the spark of creativity. Every time Captain Jean-Luc Picard faced a challenging problem on the Enterprise and sought a creative resolution from his crew, the person who proposed the successful solution – often his First Officer, "Number One" – would receive the command to "Make it so."

In a broader sense, "Make it so" embodies a spirit of innovation by encouraging immediate action and forward momentum. It suggests a willingness to embrace new ideas and technologies, and to proactively address challenges or problems. "Make it so" suggests that asking questions can lead to new ideas and innovations, similar to how necessity drives the creation of new inventions. It emphasizes the importance of curiosity and inquiry in fostering creativity and problem-solving.

In scientific research, asking questions about the natural world can lead to new discoveries and advancements. For example, asking "Why do certain plants thrive in specific environments?" could inspire research into plant genetics and environmental adaptations. Many scientific breakthroughs have been driven by questions. Another example, the question "Why does the apple fall from the tree?" led Sir Isaac Newton to develop his theory of gravity, revolutionizing physics.

In technology development, questions like "How can we make communication faster?" and "How can we improve communication between devices?" led to the invention of the telephone by Alexander Graham

Bell and later the development of wireless communication devices and smartphones.

In health care, asking questions like "How can we improve patient care and outcomes?" can lead to the development of new medical treatments, technologies, or care delivery models that enhance the quality of healthcare services.

Businesses constantly face challenges and questions like "How can we improve customer satisfaction?" or "What new markets can we tap into?" These questions drive innovation and lead to the development of new products, services, and business strategies.

Individuals often ask themselves questions like "What do I want to achieve in life?" or "How can I overcome this obstacle?" These questions inspire personal growth and development as people seek answers and strive to improve themselves.

Artists often ask themselves questions like "What emotions do I want to evoke?" or "How can I express this concept visually?" These questions guide their creative process and lead to the creation of novels, paintings, music, and other forms of art.

In each of these examples, questions serve as the spark that ignites creativity and drives innovation and progress.

Memoirist and short story writer Patricia Hampl claims that she doesn't write what she knows about; rather, she writes what she wants to know about. Her approach to writing is a reflection of a curious and exploratory mindset. By stating that she writes about what she wants to know about rather than what she already knows, she emphasizes the importance of learning and discovery in the creative process, essentially by asking questions.

Writing about what one wants to know about can also be a way to challenge oneself, push boundaries, and break out of comfort zones. It can inspire growth, creativity, and personal development as the writer engages with unfamiliar or unexplored territories.

There is no better way to turn a challenging problem or question into readiness to proceed with a proposed solution or new idea, moving from discussion or deliberation into action – to "Make it so!"

13.
Writing in the "Shadow of the Text"

The clinical equivalent of conducting psychotherapy or practicing with uncertainty.

My narrative medicine instructor encouraged our class to "write in the shadow of the text." Writing in the shadow of the text is a term that refers to the practice of writing about or interpreting a text by focusing on its hidden, underlying, or less obvious aspects. This might involve looking at subtext, implications, assumptions, or contexts that are not immediately apparent in the "surface" of the text.

In a medical context, the phrase can potentially refer to the practice of taking notes or writing about a patient's medical history, symptoms, or experiences in a way that captures not just the "hard facts" but also the less quantifiable aspects, such as emotional states, social circumstances, or implicit concerns. It is a more empathetic and holistic approach to medical documentation that can help in understanding the patient's perspective and delivering personalized care.

Grasping the viewpoint of the patient is of utmost importance in health care, yet it is often not requested or considered as much as it should be. Lewis Mehl-Madrona, MD, PhD, who is synonymous with the narrative medicine movement, remarked, "My criticism of alternative and holistic medicine resembles my thoughts about conventional medicine – that it constructs experts who are supposed to know more about the person and her condition than she does, that it purports to fix people from a position outside of them, that it fails to respect and elicit people's local knowledge about how to heal themselves."

Let's say a patient comes in with recurring headaches. The physician notes down the symptoms, frequency, intensity, and duration of the headaches, which might be considered the "text." This is the explicit information presented.

Writing in the shadow of the text, in this case, might involve jotting down additional observations or information that could be relevant, even though they are not part of the chief complaint. For instance, the physician might note that the patient appears stressed, mentions having trouble at work, and has been sleeping poorly. The physician might also record that the patient's tone changes when talking about their personal life, suggesting that there may be emotional or psychological factors contributing to their physical symptoms.

This information, captured "in the shadow" of the main text can help the physician understand the patient's situation more comprehensively and perhaps identify stress or anxiety as potential contributing factors to the headaches, which might not be immediately apparent from the "text" of the primary complaint alone.

When I first heard the phrase "writing in the shadow of the text," it evoked connotations of the color grey for me. This included: *Grey's Anatomy*, the iconic medical textbook and TV series; grey matter, a vital part of the central nervous system; and grey areas, scenarios where right and wrong are not clearly defined.

Grey areas involve diagnostic dilemmas, treatment options, ethical considerations, or areas where evidence-based guidelines are lacking or conflicting. In such instances, healthcare professionals must rely on their expertise, past experiences, and judgment to make the most beneficial decision for the patient. You could say that physicians practice in the "shadows" when symptoms are unclear, uncertain, or open to interpretation.

Conducting psychotherapy is also akin to writing in the "shadow of the text" because it involves interpreting and co-constructing meaning from the patient's narrative. The therapist listens to the patient's words, emotions, and silences, much like a writer draws from unspoken subtext and implicit themes in a story. Both processes require attending to what is present while intuitively sensing what lies beneath – hidden patterns, contradictions, or deeper truths. In this shadowed space, therapist and patient collaboratively create a "text" of understanding, re-authoring the patient's narrative in ways that foster healing and growth.

Our writing instructor concluded, "sharing our stories, our humanity, resides in those very shadows – and we are the texts."

The best way to listen to our patients and to honor them is in writing – in the "shadow of the text."

14.
Our Secret Life Comes Out in Prose and Poetry

"Don't get it right, just get it written."
— James Thurber

I was engaged in a three-way chat on WhatsApp with my narrative medicine instructor and a classmate, who was also a physician. During our discussion, I brought up the theme of *forgiveness*. This prompted our instructor to reflect on relationships, specifically the strained dynamic she shared with her older sister, which she described as "stressed."

I could deeply empathize with the harm that sibling relationships can sometimes cause. My older brother used to torment and tease me about my weight when we were young. Yet, over time, I found the strength to forgive him. The poet Jimmy Santiago Baca, who discovered poetry while imprisoned, once wrote: "Being a human being without forgiveness is like being a guitarist without fingers or being the diva without a tongue." Today, in our seventies, my brother and I are the best of friends. I couldn't sense the same kind of reconciliation between my teacher and her sister.

The conversation shifted when my classmate referenced James Thurber's short story *The Whip-Poor-Will*, published in *The New Yorker* on August 9, 1941. He described it as a story of "blame and forgiveness," though it's undeniably grim: a man, driven to madness by a whippoorwill's call, murders his wife and two servants before taking his own life.

My classmate elaborated, "Did you know James Thurber lost the sight in one of his eyes after his brother shot him with an arrow while they were playing William Tell? His brother missed the apple on his head! Years later,

Thurber wrote *The Whip-Poor-Will*. As an undergrad, I wrote a thesis on that story, but I missed the subtle irony – his brother's name was William. *Whip-poor-will*...William."

He then suggested to our instructor, "Maybe stories or poetry could be a bridge for your sister. Have you considered exploring forgiveness with her through poetry?"

Sensing the potential for our instructor to feel vulnerable or distressed, I chose not to revisit the topic of her sister. Instead, I redirected the discussion toward Thurber. I remarked, "Thurber also created Walter Mitty," a nod to his famous 1939 short story *The Secret Life of Walter Mitty*. In it, Mitty escapes his humdrum life through vivid daydreams, imagining himself as a daring pilot, a brilliant surgeon, an assassin, and a fearless soldier. "Our secret lives emerge in prose and poetry," I added, wrapping up our exchange.

Our instructor responded with a heart emoji, subtly affirming my comment. There was no further mention of forgiveness or sibling relationships.

Prose is one of the most powerful mediums to explore our secret selves. Through detailed narratives, character development, and plot, we can express our hidden desires, fears, and dreams. Prose allows us to create scenarios where we can live out these secret lives, much like Walter Mitty does in his daydreams. These narratives can be cathartic, allowing us to confront and understand our inner selves better.

Poetry, with its emphasis on emotions and imagery, can provide a more abstract and symbolic representation of our secret lives. It allows us to express our deepest emotions and thoughts in a condensed and potent form. Metaphors, similes, and other poetic devices enable us to hint at our hidden selves without explicitly stating them.

Whether through pose or poetry, the act of writing can serve as a form of self-discovery and introspection, helping us uncover our unique and hidden identities. Thurber commented: "The original of Walter Mitty is every other man I have ever known. When the story was printed in *The New Yorker*...six men from around the country, including a Des Moines dentist, wrote and asked me how I had got to know them so well. No writer can ever put his finger on the exact inspiration of any character in fiction that is worthwhile, in my estimation. Even those commonly supposed to be taken from real characters rarely show much similarity in the end."

Thurber's observation is a testament to our individuality, a distinctiveness that transcends our occupation and status in life. At the same time, all humans share similar bonds in their thinking and capacity to imagine, probably because storytelling is hardwired into our brains to some extent (refer to essay 7). Film critic David Fear wrote, "Whatever the inspiration, a huge part of what makes the short story so resonant for us card-carrying members of the Daydream Nation is the way its style replicates our mindset so accurately, dipping in and out of absurdist imaginary situations with an admirable agility."

If you're the type of person that is on the introverted side, like me, and concerned about how individuals may view you for speaking out or simply for being yourself, consider writing as an alternate way to express your authenticity and inner self. As a physician, you would do well to remember that your day-to-day experiences and interactions with patients, families, caregivers, and others connected to health care are considerably fuller and more exciting than Mitty's real life as a nebbish conscripted into chauffeuring his wife on Sunday errands.

Thurber's tragic childhood accident resulted in sympathetic ophthalmia (an inflammatory eye condition), and it almost blinded him. He admitted that writing "Whip-Poor-Will revealed his anger toward five unsuccessful eye operations. Thurber's near-blindness caused him to grow up to see the world in a bizarre and hilarious light, blurring the line between fantasy and reality in his works. However, you don't have to resort to fantasy and grandiose delusions to get by in life. Write about your encounters, don't envision them.

15.
Daydreaming and the Default Mode Network in Narrative Creation

There's a reason why it's difficult for our brains to turn off.

In the introduction to *Remapping Your Mind: The Neuroscience of Self-Transformation Through Story*, Lewis Mehl-Madrona, MD, PhD and Barbara Mainguy, MA, wrote: "We need to understand story, because story is our default mode: it is intrinsic to who we are. Story is what we use to explain our world. Story is what we use to create identity. More than that, increasingly it seems apparent that the stories we tell ourselves literally impact our health."

This husband-and-wife clinical and research duo then described the default mode network (DMN), which they claimed was a story in itself! The DMN is a network of interacting brain regions that is active when the individual is not focused on the outside world and the brain is at wakeful rest, such as during daydreaming and mind-wandering. It has been estimated that our mind spends at least 50% of the time in a state of wandering.

During these periods, the brain is often engaged in internal tasks such as recalling memories, envisioning the future, monitoring the environment, and thinking about the thoughts and perspectives of others. This is often referred to as self-referential thinking or processing, and it gives us a sense of identity and knowing who we are. The DMN is deactivated when we focus on external stimuli and the task at hand, such as reading a book or watching television.

The DMN includes areas of the brain such as the medial temporal lobe (involved in memory), the medial prefrontal cortex (involved in decision making and social interactions), and the posterior cingulate cortex/precuneus (involved in consciousness and self-awareness). Widespread connections play a role in various theories linking a malfunctioning DMN to neuropsychiatric disorders ranging from ADHD to autism to Alzheimer's disease.

The fascinating thing about the brain is that it is constantly active at a high level even when we are not engaged in intense mental work or focused on the outside world. In fact, the brain's energy consumption is increased by less than 5% of its baseline while performing a focused mental task. It may seem counterintuitive that a neural network is active during relatively restful periods, but it's not a surprise considering that other parts of the body work in a similar way.

For example, the parasympathetic nervous system (PNS) division of the autonomic nervous system is more active when the body is relaxed or at rest. The PNS slows the heart rate, decreases blood pressure, helps control breathing, and stimulates digestion and other restorative processes.

In the context of daydreaming, the DMN allows us to generate and explore scenarios and events that aren't happening in the present moment. This can aid in future planning, creative thinking, problem-solving, and developing empathy. Daydreaming can also play a significant role in creating medical narratives. There are several ways this may happen:

1. **Enhancing Empathy**: Daydreaming allows healthcare professionals to imagine themselves in their patients' shoes, which can help them better understand their experiences and feelings. This can help create a more compassionate and comprehensive narrative.

2. **Problem-Solving**: Daydreaming can aid in problem-solving and innovative thinking. It can help medical professionals to think beyond the conventional to find new solutions or treatments for their patients.

3. **Stress Relief**: Daydreaming can provide a much-needed mental break for healthcare professionals, helping them manage stress and avoid

burnout. This can enable them to maintain a clear mind and create more accurate and effective medical narratives.

4. **Memory Consolidation**: Daydreaming can help with memory consolidation, allowing for better recollection of patient histories and details, which is crucial for creating accurate medical narratives.

5. **Creative Thinking**: Daydreaming stimulates creative thinking, which can help in developing a more engaging and understandable narrative for patients, other healthcare professionals, or even for medical teaching and research.

6. **Reflection**: Daydreaming provides an opportunity for reflection, which can be crucial in understanding the different aspects of a patient's medical journey. This reflection can contribute to the creation of a holistic and personalized medical narrative.

It is important to balance daydreaming with active, focused thinking. While daydreaming can offer many benefits, it's also crucial to stay grounded in facts and details. Excessive activity in the DMN, such as during prolonged periods of daydreaming or rumination, has been linked to mental health conditions such as depression, anxiety and obsessive-compulsive disorder. So, while the DMN plays a crucial role in daydreaming and other cognitive functions, it's also important to maintain a balance between internal and external focus. Meditation and exercise are two good ways to modulate activity in the DMN and stay on an even keel.

John Sebastian penned his famous song "Daydream" in a swift 20-minute session. The song was born on a particularly gloomy rainy day when Sebastian was battling feelings of depression due to parting ways with his girlfriend for an extended period on the road. He revealed to *Hit Parader* that writing served as a therapeutic escape, preventing him from "flipping out."

While Sebastian might not have interpreted it in this manner, his excessive contemplation and daydreams about his girlfriend were causing his mood to plummet. By immersing himself in the process of writing and creating "Daydream," he managed to steer clear of spending too much unhealthy time in the DMN. Thus, it could be said that crafting "Daydream" potentially saved him from a nightmare. It's oft been quoted, "If you don't have dreams, you have nightmares."

16.
How Does the Writer's Mood Affect the Writing and Rewriting of Narratives and Memoir?

"No man ever steps in the same river twice, for it's not the same river and he's not the same man."

—Heraclitus

Kevin Pho, MD, is best known for creating and hosting the popular website KevinMD (https://www.kevinmd.com), considered social media's leading physician voice. KevinMD is my go-to website for publishing essays and op-eds. It's a safe place where healthcare providers – really anyone – can share their insight and tell their stories.

Kevin also presents podcasts and advocates for recent publications pertinent to the medical profession. I forwarded him a poem from my book *Medicine on Fire: A Narrative Travelogue*, hoping he would promote the book on his website. Kevin asked, "Do you have a narrative excerpt? I prefer those to poems."

While I'm unsure of the reason for Kevin's preference for essays over poetry, I nevertheless sent him a narrative from the book. The essay explored the idea of how the capricious nature of memory can influence the accuracy of the narrative. I sent the essay verbatim from the book, as he had asked. However, before hitting "click and send," I reviewed it once more and opted to make some slight modifications.

H. G. Wells revisited his classic *The Time Machine* 36 years after he wrote it (refer to essay 10). Looking it over once more, he decided to add a new preface, this time writing as a "mature writer." He stated that the book seemed like a "a very undergraduate performance," although he had no reservations it would outlive him, attesting to its power.

I began to wonder whether a writer's mood might affect the writing and rewriting (or revision) of narratives and memoir – and perhaps even works of fiction? I mean, life does sometimes give us second chances, and our attitudes may have changed in the interim, and along with them, our mood, outlook, and perspective. Like Wells, we may become more sophisticated in our writing approach with age.

The same is true of storytelling. It is well known that people are prone to telling the same story differently over time. Stories are rarely retold identically unless they are well rehearsed, e.g., by professional storytellers, comedians, and the like. The retelling of stories introduces a degree of emotional and cognitive coloring. Although it's unintentional, the story comes out differently the second (and third, etc.) time around. You can't step in the same river twice, paraphrasing Heraclitus.

Many factors influence the outcome of a revision, chief among them our mood – whether positive or negative, happy or depressed – as I discovered when I resent my essay to Kevin. I know from my experience that my mood – indeed, the writer's mood – can significantly influence the writing and rewriting of narratives and memoirs.

Keep in mind, I am only addressing normal variations in mood and not pathological states of mania or depression as seen in individuals who have actual mood disorders, such as bipolar disorder and major depression. Volumes have been written about the impact of mood disorders on writing, mainly their effects on the creative process – typically described as "heightened" during manic episodes – and also other aspects of writing such as productivity, content, focus, organization and perseverance.

Depression can lead to a lack of motivation, concentration, and energy, potentially causing decreased productivity. Writers with depression might struggle to maintain the effort needed to complete a writing task, particularly in the face of criticism or rejection. On the other hand, manic phases in bipolar disorder may result in increased productivity but can also lead to inconsistent and disorganized writing. during altered mood states, writers may struggle to consider the perspective of the reader, which can impact the effectiveness of their communication. When their mood is stable, writers may use their work as an outlet to retrospectively make sense of experiences when they were ill. This can lead to deeply personal, insightful, and emotionally charged writing that readers find highly engaging.

Thought disorders like schizophrenia can disrupt the logical flow of ideas, making the writing process more challenging. Individuals with schizophrenia typically display disorganized thinking, making it difficult for a writer to maintain a clear, logical narrative. This can impact the structure and coherence of their writing. That's why it is essential that individuals with mood and thought disorders receive appropriate support, including mental health treatment and possibly accommodations or adaptations in their writing process, to help them succeed in their writing endeavors.

17.
Shepherd Your Story – and Help Others Shepherd Their Own

"It's as though I get to live my life over again, but this time with meaning."
—Story Shepherd John Bibb Hickman

Stories, whether written or verbally expressed – or both – have stood the test of time. However, their legacy may be threatened by "book burnings" and other unenlightened attempts at censorship and suppressing free speech and dissenting ideas.

According to Pen America, during the first half of the 2022-23 school year there were 1,477 instances of individual books banned, affecting 874 unique titles, an increase of 28% compared to the prior six months, January-June 2022. Efforts to ban books were initiated primarily by parents, with Texas, Florida, Missouri, Utah, and South Carolina topping the list – for all sorts of reasons: LGBTQ+, religious, racial, historical, political, profanity and other types of content. Widespread attempts to categorize specific books as "harmful" and "explicit" are increasing the range of content being censored in educational institutions.

Consider the saga of *Fahrenheit 451*, a dystopian novel written by Ray Bradbury and first published in 1953. The book presents a future society where books are outlawed and "firemen" burn any that are found. The title refers to the temperature that Bradbury understood to be the autoignition point of paper.

Fahrenheit 451 stands as a warning against the dangers of a future where intellectual freedom is stifled, and conformity is enforced. Bradbury uses this narrative to champion the importance of books, individual thought, and the freedom to interpret and understand the world around us.

Bradbury was also responding to the rise of mass media, particularly television, and its potential to diminish interest in literature and reading. He feared that society could become intellectually uncurious and uninformed due to an over-reliance on simplified, quick-fix media as a source of information and entertainment, not unlike today's reliance on social media for news gathering and amusement.

Fahrenheit 451 follows Guy Montag, a fireman who burns books for a living. In contrast to a traditional fireman, Montag's job is to start fires to destroy books and the houses they are found in, rather than putting fires out. Throughout the course of the novel, Montag's dissatisfaction with his life grows, and he begins to rebel against society. He secretly collects books that he's supposed to burn, spurred on by a series of events and characters, such as his teen neighbor Clarisse who is open-minded and free-spirited, and a former English professor named Faber.

After a series of events, including the death of Clarisse, the suicide of his wife Mildred, and his own murder of his fire chief, Montag becomes a fugitive. He escapes the city, which is subsequently destroyed by an atomic bomb in a war that has been brewing throughout the novel.

Montag finds a group of educated but homeless individuals who each memorize a book to keep it alive. They welcome him, and he joins their mission to preserve knowledge. In this group, Montag finds a new sense of purpose, that of a storyteller.

Montag chooses to memorize the Book of Ecclesiastes from the Bible. The choice of this particular book is significant because Ecclesiastes discusses themes of vanity, the fleeting nature of life, and the pursuit of knowledge, all of which are central to the narrative of *Fahrenheit 451*.

The novel ends with Montag and his new companions setting off towards the ruined city with the intention of helping rebuild society from its ashes, carrying with them the hope that the knowledge and culture preserved in their memories can be used to establish a literate and thoughtful society.

A storytelling facsimile of *Fahrenheit 451* can be found in the "Story Shepherds," a real and genuine group of people from Northern Ireland who were deeply affected by the intense conflict that occurred there from the late 1960s until the Good Friday Agreement of 1998. The Good Friday Agreement, a major political development in the peace process between the Irish Republican Army (IRA) and the British government, led to the IRA announcing a ceasefire and eventually stating that its armed campaign was over.

However, the conflict, often referred to as "The Troubles," had a profound impact on people: loss of life and injury; psychological trauma; displacement; economic upheaval; and social division and a disruption of daily life. The conflict affected all aspects of life, from travel (due to road closures and checkpoints) to education (with schools often being affected by violence). The constant threat of violence created a climate of fear and tension.

More than that, the conflict exacerbated social and sectarian divisions between the Protestant unionist/loyalist community who wanted Northern Ireland to remain part of the United Kingdom, and the Catholic nationalist/republican community who wanted it to leave the UK and join a united Ireland.

Over 3,500 people were killed and thousands more were injured during this period. The victims included not just those directly involved in the conflict, but also civilians who were caught in the crossfire or targeted in attacks. The "Story Shepherds" emerged to unify healing and foster forgiveness by re-telling moving personal accounts involving themselves, family members, and acquaintances – stories capable of renewing lives, bringing meaning to suffering, and understanding among people who once were enemies and are now friends.

My writing instructor has roots in Belfast and is a huge supporter of the "Story Shepherds." She wrote, "The Story Shepherds invoke our shared ancestry of storytellers who have all explored their stories as a vital part of becoming whole. Until we look back into the labyrinth of our tale, we feel it calling to us, beckoning us to draw from it medicine we need...Even from the depths of injury and tragedy, our stories draw us out into the light we may not even feel we deserve."

My instructor encourages everyone to find their "Shepherd's Way," but she insists on one condition: "Once we have shepherd our own story, we help others shepherd their own."

18.
Scams Perpetrated on Physician Authors by Impersonators and Bad Actors

There is a high prevalence of fraud and other bad practices in and around the publishing industry.

Shortly after publishing a book, I received what seemed like a promising film adaptation offer from a reputable-sounding company. Despite initial excitement, I discovered it was a sophisticated scam. This experience taught me to stay vigilant and verify unsolicited offers – not only book and movie deals but any business promise that appeals to your ego and seems like a get-rich-quick scheme.

Many accounts similar to mine have been reported on the internet. I have a few recommendations for writers and creatives that I have adapted from the official blog of Writer Beware® by Victoria Strauss, an author on a mission "[to] shine a bright light into the dark corners of the shadow-world of literary scams, schemes, and pitfalls."

Here are some of her tips and mine:

1. **Verify identities**: Always verify the identities of individuals and companies making unsolicited offers. Cross-check their contact details and credentials through official channels. Hundreds of bona fide entities have been skillfully impersonated by bad actors representing movie companies, producers, agents, publishers, bookstores, and media companies.

2. **Consult professionals**: If approached with offers involving significant rights or financial transactions, consult with a literary agent or

legal professional before proceeding.

3. **Ask for a reality check**: Don't forget the adage that if something is too good to be true, it probably is. It's difficult to be objective about your own work, so seek the opinions of family members and trusted colleagues who don't have skin in the game. Ask them for an honest opinion about whether the offer seems real or fake and what makes your work so special that it would be singled out among a thousand others also deserving recognition.

4. **Check your ego**: While it's natural to feel flattered by interest in your work, it's essential to stay grounded. Scammers often exploit pride and excitement, so approach such offers with a healthy dose of skepticism. Remember that legitimate opportunities usually come through established channels and often involve due diligence and formal processes.

5. **Beware foreign actors**: At present, most scams impacting U.S.-based writers come from overseas – the Philippines, Pakistan, and India. They are highly predatory and may be linked to so-called "vanity publishers" using overseas employees to produce your work. It's a risk that authors take when they self-publish their writing.

6. **Keep an eye on your finances**: Scammers will try to hook you and pressure you to spend money on goods and services that may be highly overpriced, non-existent, never actually delivered, or all three. Some have the means (through leaked information) to access your online banking information and hack your account. Never provide your bank account and routing numbers to anyone other than the most trusted authorities. Do not share your bank information with your publisher unless proper fraud precautions have been established – such as in a real estate wiring transaction.

7. **Remain skeptical of unsolicited offers**: Scammers primarily acquire sensitive information by phishing through solicitation, and they

are persistent. It is extremely rare for reputable business people to contact authors out of the blue, although it sometimes happens.

8. **Reject purchase fees and requirements**: Reputable agents, publishers, and production companies should not charge you for their representation or rights to acquire your work. Do not let them sell you any type of service or refer you to any third-party company or provider you have to pay.

9. **Report suspicious activity**: Report any suspicious offers or communications to relevant authorities or industry bodies to help protect others from similar scams. Write or talk about your experience and warn your writing group or close associates to be careful and avoid these scams.

10. **Expect professionalism at all times**: Whether you are approached in writing or through a telephone call, watch out for these additional tell-tale signs. They are highly correlated with author scams:

- Form letters, mismatched fonts, pasted material, and other examples that lack personalized communication.
- Spoofed phone numbers and addresses that do not match the location of the company that the individual claims to represent.
- Over-the-top compliments and flattering and flowery praise of your work.
- Overly friendly first lines or presumptive acquaintances. ("I hope this email finds you in good health and high spirits and that you are still thriving in your personal journey.")
- A guarantee that your work has been thoroughly read and vetted by – or recommended to – company executives.
- Evidence of English as a second language or use of pronunciation applications for non-native English speakers, e.g., BoldVoice.

My fifth-grade teacher often said, "A word to the wise is sufficient," as she would admonish a student and set them straight. She believed that once warned, the student's wayward behavior would not recur. By sharing my experience, I aim to raise awareness among fellow authors and creatives, helping them avoid the scams that I have encountered.

Authors, let this be your "word."

19.
Publish or Perish Your Way to Tent City

Medical universities should strive to create a supportive and balanced academic environment.

I was corresponding with a good friend, a retired English teacher, who said he wasn't doing much writing these days. A few of his recent poems had been rejected for publication. My friend wrote, "It's a good thing I don't need to get paid for publishing it; otherwise, I might be living in a tent city."

My friend was obviously expressing frustration and disappointment with his lack of success in getting his poems published. His reference to "tent city," a term used to describe makeshift communities of homeless people living in tents, seemed a bit peculiar given that it is not necessary for him to make money from writing poetry – he and his wife live off of their investments and they are not destitute or facing financial hardship.

My friend was clearly referring to the "publish or perish" aphorism describing the pressure to publish scholarly work in order to succeed in an academic career. The phrase "publish or perish" highlights the pressure academics often face to continuously produce publishable material. If they don't, they risk their careers stagnating or ending (the "perish" part).

The phrase "publish or perish" originated in the context of academia almost 100 years ago, but its exact origins are unknown. In *The Academic Man: A Study in the Sociology of a Profession,* a 1942 book by sociologist Logan Wilson, there is a chapter on prestige and the research function. Wilson stated: "The prevailing pragmatism forced upon the academic group is that one must write something and get it into print. Situational imperatives dictate a 'publish or perish' credo within the ranks" (p. 197). However, it is unknown whether Wilson was citing or coining the phrase.

Nevertheless, the phrase "publish or perish" quickly gained widespread use and spread to academic environments worldwide. It has been both criticized and defended. Critics say it promotes quantity over quality and can lead to stress and burnout. Supporters argue that it encourages productivity and maintains a high standard of research. Regardless of these debates, the phrase "publish or perish" remains well-grounded in the lexicon and is a reality in many academic fields, including medicine.

Medical faculty members are often required to produce a significant amount of scholarly work. This includes research papers, articles, and studies published in peer-reviewed medical and scientific journals. The pressure to publish in medicine is driven by several factors. Career advancement is often tied to the quantity and quality of published work. Professors who publish regularly are more likely to receive promotions, tenure, and salary increases, although the publish or perish culture might also perpetuate gender and racial bias in academic institutions.

The reputation of a medical university is also linked to the research output of its faculty, with higher publication rates often leading to better rankings. This, in turn, attracts more funding and higher quality students.

Funding is another key driver of the "publish or perish" culture. Many grant agencies require evidence of productivity in the form of publications, so medical researchers are under pressure to publish to secure future funding. Additionally, publishing research findings is an essential part of scientific progress, allowing for the dissemination of knowledge, advances in medical science, and improvements in patient care.

However, the pressure to publish can also have negative implications. It can compromise the quality of research and lead to scientific misconduct as researchers rush the process or cut corners to meet publication demands. It can also discourage innovative but risky research projects that may not result in immediate publications. The constant pressure can also deter potential academics from pursuing a career in medical research.

The "publish or perish" culture affects both physician and non-physician faculty members in medical universities, but the impact and expectations can differ based on their roles and responsibilities.

Physicians in academic settings often have three roles: provide clinical care, teach medical students and residents, and conduct research. The pressure to publish for these physicians can be intense, as they must balance their time between patient care, teaching, administrative duties, and research. However, their clinical experiences can provide valuable insights and data for research, and their publications often focus on clinical studies and case reports that directly impact patient care. Some physicians gravitate toward clinical trials to determine the efficacy of drugs and devices.

On the other hand, non-physician faculty members, such as medical researchers or educators, may have more time dedicated to research as it is a major part of their job description. They are often expected to consistently produce research and may have more pressure to secure grant funding, which often depends on their publication record. Their research often spans basic sciences, medical education, or public health issues.

However, it is important to note that the "publish or perish" culture can lead to stress and burnout in both groups. Balancing the demands of clinical work, teaching, and research can be challenging for physician faculty, while non-physician faculty may face intense competition for grants and pressure to publish. Medical universities should therefore consider these unique pressures and work towards creating a supportive environment that values both quality and quantity in academic output.

Medical universities can take several steps in this regard. For instance, they can provide faculty with resources and training to improve their research and writing skills. This could include workshops on research methodology, statistical analysis, and scientific writing, which would help faculty produce high-quality research.

Mentorship programs can also be beneficial. Pairing junior faculty with experienced researchers can provide them with guidance and support as they navigate the academic landscape. These mentors can share their knowledge and experience, helping their mentees avoid common pitfalls and succeed in their academic endeavors.

Additionally, universities can encourage research collaboration among faculty. Fostering a collaborative, team effort rather than a competitive ("cut-throat") culture can lead to more impactful and higher quality research. This can also help distribute the research burden among several individuals, reducing the pressure on any single person.

In terms of assessing academic output, universities can move away from solely counting the number of publications. Instead, they can also consider the quality of the research, its impact on the field, and the faculty member's contribution to the research team. "One brilliant article should outweigh one mediocre book," noted cultural critic Camille Paglia.

Lastly, providing support for grant writing can also be helpful. Securing funding is a significant part of academic research and can be a major source of stress. Offering resources and assistance with grant writing can increase the chances of success and reduce the pressure on faculty.

These strategies can help medical universities create a more supportive and balanced academic environment, reducing the negative impacts of the "publish or perish" culture. It is crucial for medical universities to achieve this balance to ensure the well-being of their faculty.

20.
We Shouldn't Let Case Reports Become a Lost Art

Writing case reports requires discipline, but it leads to refined skills that can take your career to new heights.

My first published papers were case reports of interesting psychiatric patients I treated as a resident: a woman with thyroid-induced psychosis miraculously "cured" by a subtotal thyroidectomy; the first-ever report of myoglobinuric renal failure due to tardive dyskinesia; identical twins who shared the same delusions (folie à deux); and several patients suspected of having Munchausen syndrome (refer to essay 8).

However, I was advised by my chairman to never draw conclusions from a study with an "n of one," because there is considerable doubt about the value of information pertaining to only one patient. "Are the data reliable and replicable?" he asked. "Is the conclusion generalizable to other patients and populations?"

True to form, in 1984, the *American Journal of Psychiatry* decided not to publish case reports apart from brief letters to the editor deemed to have unique educational value. Other journals followed suit.

Around the turn of the century, there was backlash against the suppression of case reports. The demand for their publication increased, leading to cases reported as "clinical conferences," "perspectives," and "hindsight." The development of online publishing spearheaded the resumption of single-case reporting, with the *British Medical Journal* paving the way. The individual case report once again became a powerful tool to illustrate complex clinical decision making relevant to the practice of holistic and evidence-based medicine.

However, the rules of evidence-based medicine relegated case reports to the lowest level in the hierarchy of studies. Evidence gathered from randomized clinical trials and meta-analyses was given much more weight than information gleaned from case studies. I stood by the case report as an important source of knowledge for clinicians in their quest to better understand their patients' diagnoses and treatment options.

The learning that occurs by reading a case report is derived not only from the presentation of the case – often a *forme fruste* – but also from the case discussion. The discussion is typically enriched by an extensive search of the medical literature. The bibliography further invites clinicians to read the references to gain a deeper understanding of the clinical issues.

My flirtation with case reports was purely accidental. In my last year of medical school, while on rotation in psychiatry, I encountered a patient who seemed to have a severe infection. She was stiff, sweating, febrile, and not fully oriented. Why was she admitted to the psych unit? I thought. The referring physician included a brief note saying the patient had recently received quite a bit of antipsychotic medication for an unknown type of psychosis.

The admission note wasn't much to go on, which in itself piqued my interest. Additionally, I was beginning to develop an awareness of harmful side effects of psychiatric medications. So, I visited the medical school librarian (circa 1980, pre-Google), who kindly conducted a computerized literature search using the patient's symptoms as search terms.

The search yielded only one relevant article – a summary of the world literature, consisting of about 60 cases, of a condition called "neuroleptic malignant syndrome" (NMS). The hallmark symptoms of NMS were nearly identical to those of my patient: rigidity, hyperthermia, autonomic dysfunction, and altered mental status.

Moreover, the author of the article was a psychiatrist practicing at the Veterans Affairs (VA) hospital in my hometown of Philadelphia. What a fortunate coincidence! I called him and explained the nature of the case. He recommended that I withhold all psychotropic medication and treat the patient supportively. Following his advice, the patient recovered in about a week.

I wrote a paper describing the diagnosis and treatment of NMS, and it won second place in a residents' writing competition sponsored by the Philadelphia County Medical Society. The case was eventually published in *Psychiatric Annals*, along with another case of NMS I encountered during my residency.

I arranged a meeting with the VA psychiatrist and proposed the idea for a book about NMS and related conditions, such as heatstroke, malignant hyperthermia, serotonin syndrome, and lethal catatonia. The book was well received, and a second edition was published 14 years later as new information and research became available.

Today, the symptoms of NMS are stated as a precaution in virtually all journal advertisements and television commercials marketing medication for depression, bipolar disorder, and schizophrenia. It is gratifying to know that alerting patients to this very serious condition was sparked by a single case report culminating in a textbook.

Contrary to medical advice, I sometimes urge medical students and residents to "look for zebras," or at least research and write about patients with mysterious illnesses or conditions that stymie them. Learning how to write case reports should not become a lost art. Including case reports as publications in one's CV will command attention in competitive residency and job markets.

To be publication worthy, case reports should contain the patient's informed consent and fulfill one or more of the following criteria:

- Establish a clear purpose and elucidate teaching points or "take-aways."
- Describe a "first" or something new and unique – for example, a disease or observation.
- Report unusual therapeutic drug effects.
- Alert clinicians to serious, potentially fatal, adverse reactions and complications.
- Provide a useful clinical pearl, acronym, or mnemonic.

I wouldn't have been as attuned to patient nuances had I not first dabbled in single case methodology and had the discipline to write about my patients. Publishing a case report, especially early in a physician's career, is a scholarly activity that positions a doctor to become a "triple threat" – an educator, clinician, and researcher.

21.
The Importance of Plain Language in Writing and Medical Practice

Find common ground in the doctor-patient relationship.

Comedy legend Joan Rivers was best known for asking her audiences "Can we talk?" – a euphemism for miscommunication and misunderstanding between people. Several experiences early in my career taught me the value of communicating with patients on their terms. I fear many doctors learn this lesson the hard way, because medical training emphasizes the importance of diagnosis and treatment, often neglecting interpersonal and cultural aspects of the doctor-patient relationship.

I found this to be true in my third year of medical school, soon after I began my clinical clerkships. I was working in the emergency department (ED) of a children's hospital, and I was evaluating a child with a rash. I was pretty sure the rash was impetigo, and after getting a thumb's up from the ED attending, I blurted to the father, "Your daughter has impetigo."

The father became concerned, and in a worried tone asked, "Can you break that down for me?" I didn't stop to think about the consequences of my actions – diagnosing his daughter in a straightforward manner by sight alone, without taking a history, and using a diagnostic term he did not comprehend. I should have listened to his concerns and then explained she had a common rash seen in children her age, that it was called impetigo, and it was easily treatable.

I talked way over his head and caused unnecessary alarm. I vowed never to let that happen again. Since the incident, I made conscious attempts to use plain language with patients and families. If appropriate, I also made "small talk" to try and put patients at ease.

It wasn't until my final year in medical school, however, that I fully appreciated the fact that communication is a two-way street. I was making progress in relating to patients on their level, but it didn't occur to me that patients may have a language all their own that *I* may not understand.

One day I was evaluating a man in his late 50s. He had diabetes, and his glucose was poorly controlled. I had a conversation with him about how to take better control of his blood sugar. I made a few modifications to his therapy (with the approval of my preceptor), and then I asked whether he had any questions.

"Well doc," he replied, "can you help me with my nature?"

I looked at the man incredulously and asked him to repeat the question.

"My nature — what can you do for my nature," the man repeated.

I simply didn't understand, and I asked him once more to explain. I could tell he was becoming frustrated and angry, so I left the exam room and summoned my preceptor. My preceptor told me that the term "nature" was commonly used by men in his culture as a synonym for sexual functioning. The patient was trying to tell me he had erectile dysfunction, most likely due to diabetes.

Rather than spare the gentleman embarrassment, I added to it through my lack of cultural awareness and insensitivity to his anguish. I learned that patients may attach special meaning to symptoms and suffering. If I was to become a good doctor, I had to better understand the contexts of meaning for interpreting illness.

My final lesson in communication occurred when I was a first-year resident working in a "walk-in" clinic – a section of the ED designated for non-emergent medical problems. I picked up the patient's chart and read the chief complaint: "sore on head." I opened the exam room door and introduced myself, simultaneously scanning the young man's head for a sore.

I didn't see it.

"Show me the sore," I said to the patient. He nonchalantly dropped his pants and pulled down his underwear to show me the sore on his "head."

"Oh, that head!" The situation called for penicillin – not a bandage.

The Plain Writing Act of 2010 requires the federal government to issue public documents, such as tax returns, federal college aid applications, and Veterans Administration forms, in simple, easy-to-understand language. The Act defines "plain writing" as "writing that is clear, concise, well-organized and follows other best practices appropriate to the subject or field and intended audience. Because medical practice is highly regulated by the government, it can be argued that the requirement to use plain language extends to physicians, especially their written communications and instructions to patients.

Of course, there are times when it may not be possible or even desirable to use plain language – for example, when dictating medical reports, operative notes, and consultations to other physicians. However, this does not excuse errors in documents due to unintelligible dictation or technical terms "lost in translation" during transcription. Medical records should be reviewed and corrected when they contain inaccuracies or missing fields, including summaries and progress notes produced by artificially intelligent scribes.

Imagine my surprise after reading a patient's history in which it was reported she had made a suicide "jester" (instead of gesture). Such mistakes are no laughing matter. Hundreds of thousands of people die each year due to medical errors resulting from miscommunication. Improving communication between doctors, and between doctors and patients, is at the root of virtually all quality improvement initiatives.

The internet has made it easy for professional organizations and physicians to communicate and share information quickly to reach millions of people. However, a *JAMA* study showed that patient education materials contained in the websites of 16 medical specialties were either too complex or suffered from a lack of readability, making them difficult for patients to comprehend and potentially contributing to poor health.

I'd like to think that, if I decide to practice again, my experiences as a younger physician, plus those in the pharmaceutical industry, will have strengthened my communication skills. I've learned valuable lessons at the bedside as well as writing educational material for patients while working in pharma, including information destined for consumers searching the internet.

I use simple words and phrases. I aim for a sixth grade reading level. I avoid the use of unfamiliar scientific or medical terms, and I never use complex language or, alternatively, language that "dumbs down" information to the point where medical accuracy is lost. It is important to strike the right balance between simplicity and complexity by providing patients sufficient yet not overly detailed information.

Patients want answers to their problems delivered in a clear, unhurried manner. Overly scientific and technical medical explanations tend to create fear, anxiety, or confusion, causing a disconnection in the doctor-patient relationship. It's not uncommon for patients to discard information they find unusable, ultimately creating more work for physicians to develop positive relationships.

The answer to Joan Rivers' exhortation "Can we talk?" is "Yes" if doctors appear concerned and interested, take the time to listen before pronouncing judgment, attempt to understand symptoms as patients experience them, and translate the language of medicine into terms patients can understand.

22.

Someone Called Me "Boswell." It Was a Compliment of the Highest Order

"A man should keep his friendships in constant repair."
— James Boswell, from *Life of Samuel Johnson*

Steven Sharfstein, MD, MPA, is among the most prominent American living psychiatrists. A former president of the American Psychiatric Association and CEO of the venerable Sheppard Pratt Health System in Baltimore, Maryland, Sharfstein was a friend in need during a dark and turbulent period in my career.

I came to know Steve – it took me a few years to develop the chutzpah to call him by his first name – through writing. Steve was the editor of a column in the journal *Hospital and Community Psychiatry*, which later became *Psychiatric Services*. The column, "Economic Grand Rounds," was a semi-regular feature about managed care and health economics.

Over the years I wrote about a half-dozen articles for the column. However, Steve always attached his name to the articles in his capacity as editor, and he would introduce each article with some personal reflections. As CEO of a large health system, with considerable experience in economics, I suppose he deserved to be a co-author on these articles even though I did most of the writing.

Steve and I corresponded by postal mail in the days before the internet. I would mail him my manuscripts and he would make some brief comments for me to incorporate in a revision. This went on for a couple of years. One day, when I received his suggestions for my revision, he addressed me "Dear

Boswell." I had no clue who or what he was referring to. I had to research the origin of the salutation and the name "Boswell." Here is what I found.

Samuel Johnson was an esteemed writer and critic of the 18th century best known for *A Dictionary of the English Language*, published in 1755, James Boswell, a lawyer, was best known for his biography of Johnson, titled Life of Samuel Johnson.

Boswell first met Johnson in 1763, in a bookshop, and despite an initial awkward encounter, they soon developed a close friendship. Boswell was 22 years old at the time, while Johnson was 53. Despite the age difference and their contrasting personalities – Johnson being a moral and literary authority, and Boswell being known for his social lifestyle and personal indiscretions –they found common ground in their shared love for literature and conversation.

Boswell visited Johnson regularly in London and they traveled together in Scotland. During their time together, Boswell meticulously recorded Johnson's conversations and opinions on a wide array of subjects. These detailed accounts formed the basis of his biography of Johnson.

Life of Samuel Johnson, published in 1791, seven years after Johnson's death, is considered a seminal work in the genre of biography. Boswell's detailed and vivid depiction of Johnson's character, mannerisms, and intellect, as well as his personal and professional life, has made it one of the most celebrated biographies in English literature.

Their relationship was one of mutual admiration and respect. Johnson appreciated Boswell's vivacity, wit, and curiosity, while Boswell revered Johnson's intellect and moral authority. Their friendship, despite its unusual dynamics, has given the world a rich and detailed account of one of the 18th century's most prominent literary figures.

Essentially, Boswell's biography immortalized Johnson as one of the most colorful and fascinating figures in English literature, while also cementing their bond for posterity. My association with Steve didn't approach those monumental levels, however, I eventually comprehended why he viewed me as his "Boswell" – I was responsible for the writing, while he basked in the glory and fame!

Steve was not just a colleague, but a close friend, and our bond extended beyond the realm of writing. In the late 1990s, my career was a rollercoaster of instability. I found myself hopping from one job to another, each proving to be more disheartening than the last. I was desperate for a change, a fresh start in a new city. The time had come to bid farewell to the City of Brotherly Love, a place where it seemed neither of us had any more affection to offer.

I called Steve on the phone. I explained my situation. He said, "Sure, drive down [to Baltimore] tomorrow. I'll set up some interviews [for possible employment at Sheppard Pratt Hospital]."

The idea of relocating and beginning afresh consumed my thoughts. The subsequent day, I embarked on a 90-mile journey that felt more like fleeting moments than a couple of hours. Steve and I had conversations at the day's start and finish, with interviews and lunch filling the intervening time.

Steve phoned early the next day. "Art, they loved you," he said. "The only problem is, we don't have a job for you right now." I thanked him and we agreed to keep in touch.

Not long after, I was offered a significant role in a health insurance company located in the Midwest. Although it was more distant from Philadelphia than I would have preferred, it was the optimal career decision at that time. This move eventually paved the way for a 12-year tenure in the pharmaceutical sector and a triumphant return to Philadelphia under much more favorable conditions.

Meanwhile, I wrote a couple more articles for *Psychiatric Services*. As usual, Steve edited and co-authored them. He continued to address me as "Boswell" in our correspondence. It was deeply rewarding to have my observations, insights, and writing abilities recognized by someone of Steve's standing, even if he did claim a portion of the credit.

Labeling me "Boswell" was a compliment of the highest order.

23.
Writers: Beware of Lies, Damned Lies, and Statistics

Understand common pitfalls underlying cause-and-effect relationships before casting them in stone.

Cause-and-effect relationships – where a particular trigger, like a disease, condition, or treatment, directly results in a specific outcome – are a staple topic for healthcare journalists and science writers. It is well stablished, for example, that smoking causes lung cancer. Similarly, it is well-documented that regular, heavy alcohol consumption directly leads to liver cirrhosis. However, in the realm of medicine, most associations are not black and white.

We usually circumvent or downplay cause-and-effect relationships by using phrases like "associated with," "linked to" and "tied to" to denote there is a correlation or relationship between two factors yet we are unable to definitively establish causality. For instance, a sedentary lifestyle is often associated with heart disease. This means that a higher incidence of heart disease is observed in people who lead an inactive lifestyle, but it does not necessarily establish that a sedentary lifestyle is the direct cause of heart disease. Other factors may also contribute to the development of this condition.

Similarly, high stress levels are linked to insomnia. Although people with high stress levels often suffer from insomnia, it is not definitively proven that stress is the direct cause of insomnia, as other factors could also be involved. We might also say that high sugar consumption is associated with obesity. While there is a correlation between the two, it cannot be definitively said that high sugar consumption is the sole or primary cause of obesity, as there are many other contributing factors such as physical inactivity, genetics, and other dietary habits.

Therefore, the difference between cause and effect and phrases like "associated with" and "tied to" essentially lies in the strength and certainty of the relationship. Cause and effect indicate a direct and certain relationship, while "associated with" and "linked to" indicate a correlation or consistent relationship, but not necessarily a direct causal one.

Historically, there are several notable examples where cause and effect relationships in medical science were later proven to be incorrect. One such example is the miasma theory, which proposed that diseases like cholera and the Black Death resulted from "miasma" or bad air. This theory was eventually replaced by the germ theory of disease, which identified specific microorganisms as the true cause of these illnesses.

Another misconception involved stomach ulcers. For a long time, stress and spicy foods were believed to be the primary cause of these ulcers. However, this understanding was revolutionized in the 1980s when two Australian scientists discovered that the bacterium Helicobacter pylori was actually responsible for most stomach ulcers, not stress or diet.

A more recent and well-known example involves the alleged link between the MMR vaccine (measles, mumps, rubella) and autism. In 1998, a study suggested this link, leading to widespread fear and a drop in vaccination rates. However, the study was later retracted due to serious procedural errors, undisclosed financial conflicts of interest, and ethical violations. Numerous subsequent studies have consistently found no connection between the MMR vaccine and autism. Once debunked, however, falsehoods may linger. For example, Robert F. Kennedy, Jr.'s strident opposition to vaccines was echoed by Donald Trump, who endorsed not only conspiracy theories about their safety but also RFK, himself, as secretary of

Health and Human Services.

These examples underscore the importance of rigorous scientific research and the practice of evidence-based medicine. They serve as reminders that our understanding of medical cause and effect relationships can change and evolve based on new evidence.

Journalists often rely on the information and language used in scientific research studies, and they commonly use phrases like "associated with" and "linked to" when writing headlines. This can sometimes contribute to misunderstandings about scientific research and the role of causation in the findings.

The Association of Health Care Journalists' guidance on covering research studies actually aims for wording that suggests a less direct relationship. Creating headlines can be a challenging task as journalists need to strike a balance between accurately conveying the nuances of scientific research and making the information accessible and understandable to a broad audience.

Any discussion of causation must address the crucial role of statistics in medical research. They provide a rigorous framework for inferring cause and effect relationships from observational data. However, statistics may be difficult to understand, and they can be misleading if not used appropriately.

In fact, one of the most common pitfalls in interpreting statistical results is confusing correlation with causation. Just because two variables are correlated does not mean that one causes the other. For instance, a statistical analysis might find a correlation between ice cream sales and drowning incidents. However, it would be incorrect to conclude that ice cream causes drowning. The two are correlated because both increase during the summer months.

Another key factor in interpreting statistical results is the sample size used in the study. If the sample size is small, the results may not be reliable or applicable to a larger population. For example, a study concluding a drug's effectiveness based on a sample size of ten people might produce different results when tested on a larger, more diverse group. New FDA guidance aims to increase diversity in clinical trials, ensuring that the data collected is more representative of the patients who will use the medication. This all but guarantees a different approach to the statistical analysis of results.

Visual representations of data, such as graphs and charts, can also be misleading if manipulated. For example, changing the scale of a graph can either exaggerate or minimize apparent differences, leading to misinterpretation of the data. Numerical differences in outcomes unsupported by statistically significant "p" values should not be construed as valid claims of superiority.

Selection bias is another potential issue, occurring when the sample used in a study does not accurately represent the population it is intended to represent. This can result in skewed results that may not apply to the broader population.

Lastly, confounding variables that are not accounted for in a study can affect the outcome. For example, if a study finds a correlation between coffee drinking and lung cancer but fails to consider that coffee drinkers might also be more likely to smoke, the results could be misleading.

In sum, while statistics are a critical tool in medical research used to prove causation, their use and interpretation must be done with caution to avoid these common pitfalls. Rigorous study design, peer review, and replication of results are crucial in ensuring reliability and validity in scientific research.

The phrase "lies, damned lies, and statistics" is often attributed to Mark Twain, who used it in his autobiography. However, Twain himself, credited it to British Prime Minister Benjamin Disraeli, although there's no record of

Disraeli using the phrase.

The phrase suggests that statistics can be manipulated or misrepresented to support any argument, even a false one. It underscores the idea that while statistics can be powerful tools for understanding data and trends, they can also be misused to mislead or confuse individuals and demonstrate causality when none exists. The phrase serves as a cautionary reminder to critically evaluate statistical claims and to consider the source of data and analytical methods used to evaluate the data before assuming cause and effect and publishing the results.

24.
Overcoming Writer's Block

"Writing about a writer's block is better than not writing at all."
— Charles Bukowski

Bob Dylan took a seat at the piano at a concert in Philadelphia during the seventh leg (Fall 2023) of his two-year worldwide "Rough and Rowdy Ways" tour. He claimed to be at a loss for words. "What's the matter with me?" he asked. "I don't have much to say."

Those are the opening lines of "Watching the River Flow," the 1971 song that appeared on his "Greatest Hits Vol. II" album. The song is allegedly about finding peace with writer's block. I have difficulty believing that Dylan was blocked. More likely, as legend has it, the lyrics were hastily written in a New York recording studio with backing musicians in tow impatiently waiting to lay down a tune.

Drummer Jim Keltner recalled, "I remember Bob ... had a pencil and a notepad, and he was writing a lot. He was writing these songs on the spot in the studio, or finishing them up at least." Writer's block? Ha, ha! What some authors would give to be as prolific as Dylan.

Writer's block has likely existed since the dawn of writing, but the term itself was only coined in 1947 by the famous psychiatrist Edmund Bergler. In 1950, Bergler published a paper titled "Does 'Writer's Block' Exist?" He answered in the affirmative and labeled writer's block a "neurotic disease." Norman Mailer quipped, "Writer's block is only a failure of the ego," suggesting that all writing problems are psychological problems, stemming primarily from a fear of being judged.

The truth is, writer's block can be brought on by various factors, including stress, self-doubt, lack of inspiration, or external pressures. Paraphrasing J.K Rowling, the thing that is most wonderful and terrifying to writers is a blank page. She and many authors are all too familiar with the situation where an individual, particularly a writer, is unable to produce new work or experiences a creative slowdown. Every writer has been there; it's inevitable, really. Many have shared their experiences and strategies for overcoming it. Here are a few suggestions from physicians who have become stuck at writing:

Danielle Ofri, MD, PhD, shared that her writing process includes periods of frustration and stagnation. She emphasized that writing is hard work and often requires pushing through these difficult periods.

Atul Gawande, MD, MPH, has talked about the importance of discipline and routine in writing. He sets aside specific times for writing and sticks to this schedule, which can help push through periods of low inspiration or productivity.

Suzanne Koven, MD, MFA, a primary care physician and writer-in-residence at Massachusetts General Hospital, has discussed how she uses her experiences with patients to fuel her writing. When facing writer's block, drawing from real-life experiences can provide a wealth of material.

Abraham Verghese, MD, MFA, said in an interview that writing, much like medicine, requires practice and dedication. He suggested that persistent writing, even when it feels challenging, can help overcome periods of writer's block.

A good overview of writer's block was published by Patricia Huston, MD, MPH in *Canadian Family Physician*. Here are some insights gleaned from that article:

1. **Embrace the Process**: Many physician authors emphasize the importance of viewing writing as a process, not a one-time event. They suggest accepting writer's block as a normal part of that process – not a failure – and breaking down the work into small, manageable tasks.

2. **Write Regularly**: Physician authors often recommend establishing a regular writing routine, even in the midst of a busy medical practice. This helps to keep the writing muscles strong and can help overcome periods of block.

3. **Use Clinical Experiences as Inspiration**: As physicians, they often draw on their clinical experiences for inspiration. This can help to bypass writer's block as they always have a rich source of stories and ideas from their daily practice.

4. **Peer Support and Collaboration**: Some physician authors find that discussing their ideas with colleagues or co-authors can help break through periods of writer's block. This can provide fresh perspectives and stimulate new ideas.

5. **Continuing Education and Learning**: Physician authors are lifelong learners. Engaging in ongoing education, attending conferences, or reading medical literature can provide new ideas and inspiration, helping to overcome writer's block. Education has been my salvation. I told my narrative medicine instructor that one of the reasons I wanted to enroll in the program was to be exposed to new material that I could incorporate into my writing. Both the readings and the class discussions proved bountiful.

6. **Mindfulness and Stress Management**: Physician authors also recognize the impact of stress on creativity. Many recommend mindfulness practices, such as meditation or yoga, to manage stress and maintain mental clarity, thereby helping to overcome writer's block.

When I draw a blank at writing, I occupy my time with something else, usually listening to music. I don't worry about not being able to write. Hugh

MacLeod, author of *Ignore Everybody*, observed: "Writer's block is just a symptom of feeling like you have nothing to say, combined with the rather weird idea that you should feel the need to say something. Why? If you have something to say, then say it. If not, enjoy the silence while it lasts. The noise will return soon enough."

Of course, Dylan's comments to the Philadelphia concert-goers were not meant to be serious. In his 80s, at the tail end of a monumental career, he still has plenty to write about as well as a justified belief that his new material stands tall alongside the pillars of his celebrated catalog.

25.
Should You Publish Your Narrative?

Simply telling your story may be powerful enough.

I don't like being rejected. Who does? But I got a real chuckle when I received a rejection letter from an editor affiliated with Doximity, a website repository for doctors' essays and "Op-Meds." The letter read:

"Thanks for your submission. It looks like you have another article about narrative medicine already in the pipeline to be published, and we don't want to oversaturate that subject, especially by the same author. We will pass on publication of this piece, but welcome you to subject (sic) other works, especially if they are not on narrative medicine."

The title of the article was "Why Aren't You Writing?" It was an essay written to encourage physicians to write expressively about their encounters – with patients, peers, trainees – anything to take their mind off the drudgery of everyday practice and to help them reduce stress. Do you see the irony here? I wrote an essay on the topic of "writing," suited for a website that invites written material from physicians, and my piece was rejected precisely because the essay was about writing! Furthermore, the letter was unsigned, and I suspect that the editor made a major Freudian slip when they wrote "subject" instead of "submit." Was I "subjecting" the editor to a narrative so unpleasant that they did not even want to attach their name to the rejection letter?

I hope not.

This brings me to the main message I want to leave with readers: write, write, write. And then write some more. There were many subjects I wanted to tackle in writing Section 1 of this book, but the chief objective was to encourage physicians – indeed, anyone remotely connected to health care – to write. Write for nourishment. Write for healing. Write for your patients. Write for any reason you want to write. Capture your thoughts in a journal and write later if you don't have the time now.

And don't be afraid of rejection.

Most of you have heard the famous Michael Jordan quote about failure. It's so good, I want you to read it again, or perhaps for the first time:

> *"I've lost almost 300 games. Twenty-six times, I've been trusted to take the game winning shot and missed. I've failed over and over and over again in my life. And that is why I succeed."*

I've lost count of the number of times my writing has been rejected for publication. Several times I've thought my essays were the right stuff for *JAMA*'s column "A Piece of My Mind," a column "devoted to telling stories about the joys, challenges, and hidden truths of practicing medicine in the modern era." I have been reading that column for a long time and I admire those successful *JAMA* authors whose narratives are chosen for publication. I want to be one of them.

Certainly, not everything I've written is *JAMA* quality, but I believe some were good candidates. Over the past five years I have submitted no less than a dozen essays to *JAMA* for consideration in "A Piece of My Mind," and every one of them has been rejected, all with the same form letter:

"Dear Dr Lazarus:

We have now completed our review of your manuscript. I am sorry to inform you that we will not be able to publish the manuscript.

Every year we receive hundreds of manuscripts. Criteria for determining acceptance include priority, originality, quality, and appeal for our general medical audience. Unfortunately, your manuscript was judged by the editors not to have met the criteria necessary for publication in *JAMA*.

We were pleased to have had the opportunity to review your work. Thank you for thinking of *JAMA*.

Sincerely yours,

Deputy Editor"

Letters like these won't deter me from writing. I'll keep at it and try to publish my essays somewhere else. I'll find a home for them somewhere, even if I have to publish them myself on Medium, bypassing editors.

My strong will and inner drive to publish articles led medical students and residents to call me "Article" Lazarus, and I achieved much publication success throughout my career. I found that taking things easier and ridding myself of publication envy tempered my reaction to editors who rejected my manuscripts. It may sound counter to all I have said so far, but I don't want to leave you with the impression that publication is the main goal of writing narratives – it's not! It's nice to publish, but it's not critical or even desirable in some instances. If you're writing for yourself, for your own therapy, to enhance your well-being, to inform patients, to educate the public, then publication is secondary.

There are other ways to share your written work without actually publishing it, for example, through storytelling. Danish author Isak Dinesen (Karen Blixen), author of *Out of Africa* and other novels, remarked: "To be a person is to have a story to tell." Somehow, storytelling has become a lost art, or at least stories haven't received the credit they deserve as a legitimate path to healing. Telling stories helps us heal as we wind our way through illness, trauma, and loss. Stories help us reframe our struggles, and they can transform our lives and the lives of others.

I would encourage you to get more involved in storytelling. Here are some venues for storytelling (spoken or interactive) rather than publishing:

1. **Storytelling Events**: Platforms like *The Moth* or TEDx talks.
2. **Workshops**: Writing or reflection sessions in schools, hospitals, or communities.
3. **Conferences**: Professional gatherings with storytelling sessions or panel discussions.
4. **Support Groups**: Sharing personal narratives in health-related or community-based groups.
5. **Classrooms**: Teaching through personal or historical stories.
6. **Social Media Live Sessions**: Platforms like Instagram Live or YouTube for interactive storytelling.
7. **Theater or Performances**: Storytelling through monologues or plays.
8. **Podcasts**: Live or semi-structured interviews or storytelling formats.
9. **Oral History Projects**: Sharing personal or community narratives for preservation or impact.
10. **Cultural Events**: Storytelling circles, festivals, or heritage days.

There is no doubt stories are powerful.
Publishing them is optional.

SECTION 2

The Five-Minute Narrative: Insights for Today's and Tomorrow's Doctors

FOR MEDICAL STUDENTS

26.
Is it Noble or Selfish to Never Practice Medicine After Getting a Medical Degree?

Non-traditional careers can be an alternative to practicing medicine, although opinions are divided.

A Harvard medical school student realized in his third year that he had lost his desire to become a doctor. Nevertheless, the student decided to complete his fourth year and obtain his MD degree. The student is now planning for a career in pharma or even comedy. Some individuals who read his online essay found the student's decision-making comical in itself. Overall, their comments were evenly divided about the student's virtues and next moves.

Before exploring readers' reactions, we ought to know something about this student's reasons for opting out of the medical profession. The student wrote: "Reflecting on the elements that brought me down, I felt sadness for my patients' health, particularly when it seemed their condition could not be cured or treated effectively; disappointment over the influence of insurance coverage in determining which treatments patients received; frustration at the amount of documentation, which seemed to take precedence over time spent with patients; and discouraged by the overall environment where it seemed hospital personnel did not feel valued or happy to be there."

Let's not dwell on the merits of the student's reasons and instead dive right into readers' reactions to it, whether they shamed or commended him on his decision. I divided the comments into "selfish" and "noble." Here is a sample:

Selfish
- How did this individual get into medical school not knowing his passions? Why did he apply when still intellectually and emotionally immature?
- As someone involved in teaching students and residents throughout my career, I know that an incredible amount of time and resources are devoted to educating doctors, and I find it very distressing when someone uses those resources and never provides care, especially when the provider shortage is so bad.
- Some other student could have really made something of the spot at Harvard medical, but now society is deprived of those benefits. This seems like a very narcissistic thing to do.
- You can be humorous with a bachelor's degree.
- It is somewhat revealing that the [student] states he went into medicine to help others, and yet all the career choices he now describes are designed to help him.
- Now there's comedy. Joining up with the pharmaceutical industry that puts sales above well-being. Trying to advertise the latest and greatest (and most expensive) alternatives to disease management and shying away from promoting healthy behaviors.
- You didn't have the right stuff.

Noble
- With the pharmaceutical path, you may be able to help countless more people than you could have with the conventional MD route.
- Sounds like the smartest man in the room to me: Do what makes you happy! And avoid the EMR cash register and hamster wheel.
- If working with patients and practicing medicine is still a passion, consider using your skills and knowledge at a free clinic; if comedy

is your passion, instead, enjoy yourself!
- Follow your heart, and the mind will be of great service to others.
- Everything he says is true. We went into medicine to help people and make the world a better place. But it seems that everything is more important than the patient.
- Good luck! It just proves that there is no other type of study/education that opens so many possibilities as medicine. Good for you!
- I hope he's finding fulfillment outside the traditional med school to residency pathway, and I'm happy that he's thoughtfully making the best choices for him.

The comments do not provide a consensus on whether it is selfish or noble to never practice medicine after medical school. One commentator – not the only one – was able to see the argument philosophically from both sides, writing, "Let's not shame people into staying where they deeply do not wish to be or condemn them based on good faith decisions made when they didn't fully understand what they were getting into."

I think this commentator made many good points, so I decided to quote him entirely: "The practical realities of clinical practice as a physician must be experienced to fully appreciate [them]. Pursuing and, if ultimately admitted, getting through medical school is something of a leap of faith for many. Sometimes it turns out to be a bad fit, a realization that may dawn after committing to a lot of debt. Of course, it rankles some given that accepting admission indirectly crowds someone else out (of this scarce resource) and doesn't provide the expected societal return on investment of a practicing clinician. On the other hand, do any of us want a physician who chronically doesn't want to be in that role? He may yet apply his education and degree profitably outside of clinical practice."

Many years ago, I conducted a small study showing that over 90% of students who matriculated in two U.S. medical schools (Temple University and the University of Pennsylvania) graduated in four years (consecutively). This percentage is in line with the Association of American Medical Colleges, which found that 4-year graduation rates ranged from 81.7% to 84.1%. After six years, allowing for an interrupted education, the average graduation rate was 96.0%.

Reasons for dropping out of medical school can be diverse, but common ones include academic struggles, financial pressures, personal health or family issues, lack of interest, or, in this instance, a desire to pursue a different career path. It is important to note that the majority of dropout causes are non-academic.

After leaving medical school, former students may pursue a range of alternate career paths. Some may choose to continue their education in a related field, such as public health, biomedical sciences, or healthcare administration. Others may decide to enter the workforce directly, taking jobs in health care, education, or research. Some will pursue careers distant from medicine or unrelated to it.

Perhaps this student will follow in the footsteps of the Monty Python actor Graham Chapman (1941 to 1989), who turned down a career as a doctor to be a writer and comedian. I wish this student well, and I do not begrudge him for nearly forcing me to go to Mexico for medical school.

I never would have had a shot at Harvard anyway.

27.
How Will Tomorrow's Medical Students be Different?

New skills before and during medical school may enhance diversity and development.

The future of medical students appears promising and challenging at the same time. While there will be abundant opportunities for medical students to explore various fields of medicine, they will be challenged by high stress levels, financial burden, and unprecedented competition for prestigious residencies. How will they fare? In what ways will tomorrow's medical students be different than past generations? Here is a brief overview of what medical school applicants can expect, and how their training will provide an advantage over previous graduates, in my opinion.

A main advantage comes from training prior to matriculation into medical school. Many of the standards for acceptance into medical school by which my generation (Baby Boomers) and others were judged are no longer relevant. The soft sciences – as opposed to the hard sciences – now have standing in premedical curricula, especially courses in psychology and sociology. At Philadelphia area medical schools, for example, calculus is required at only one of eight MD or DO granting institutions (Penn State).

The Association of American Medical Colleges (AAMC) added a psychology-sociology ("psych-sosh") section to its MCAT standardized admissions exam in 2015. The revised MCAT reflects the importance of learning how to think and solve problems, with more questions requiring that future doctors use analytical skills rather than simply memorize material. Prerequisite courses in the social sciences may also yield students who are emotionally intelligent as well as clinically competent.

A study showed that physicians trained in my era – those graduating college between 1955 and 1982 – reported that their greatest unmet need was "skill with people," and my peers wished they had taken more courses in art, history, literature, and music while in college. Nowadays, some of those subjects are expected if students want to earn a spot in medical school. After decades of welcoming science nerds, medical educators have finally placed more emphasis on the humanities in medicine.

The AAMC has also created an optional exam to evaluate the "situational judgment" of students applying to medical school. The Professional Readiness Exam, formerly known as the AAMC Situational Judgment Test, consists of 30 hypothetical scenarios and 186 related questions that test the effectiveness of students' remedies to hypothetical situations encountered in the classroom and practice. The appropriateness of students' responses is a proxy for their readiness to enter medical school, as determined across eight core competencies such as service orientation, cultural competence, and teamwork.

Typical dilemmas presented to students include: (1) how to deal with a classmate who violates patient privacy on social media; (2) how to ensure a patient's cultural customs are respected in the event something unexpected occurs following surgery; (3) how to seek help when the stress of a clerkship in emergency medicine is beginning to affect sleep and judgment; (4) how to address a lecturer who is quick to dismiss multiple valid perspectives on a subject; and (5) how to deal with a classmate who has assumed a deceased immigrant was "undocumented," or a person's stomach pain was fabricated because they were homeless.

Another similar test, made by Toronto-based Acuity Insights, is called Casper. This assessment evaluates aspects of students' social intelligence and professionalism such as ethics, empathy, problem-solving, and collaboration. The evaluation offers admissions assessments that give each applicant the opportunity to showcase their attributes beyond their grades and to differentiate themselves from other applicants.

The removal of affirmative action admission policies by the Supreme Court of the U.S. (SCOTUS) in 2023 has not deterred medical schools from efforts to select diverse students, deemed necessary to reduce health disparities. Conducting holistic reviews of applicants and searching for unique personal characteristics complies with the SCOTUS ruling and supports diversity. In addition, some medical schools have instituted community outreach and "pipeline" programs to attract a more diverse applicant pool.

The University of California Davis School of Medicine has maintained a remarkably diverse class of students by assessing their socioeconomic status rather than their race and ethnicity (affirmative action admissions have been banned in California public colleges since 1996). A heterogeneous workforce has been shown to improve patient outcomes and increase trust in the doctor-patient relationship. Furthermore, teaching diversity, equity, and inclusion across medical school campuses fosters a sense of belonging among staff and faculty and the patients they serve.

Tomorrow's medical students will be vastly different from their predecessors not only due to their premedical training and selective screening for admission, but also due to changes in medical education methods, evolving technological advancements, and the continuously shifting healthcare landscape.

With the rise of digital health technologies such as telemedicine, artificial intelligence (AI), and machine learning, future medical students will be better technologically equipped. They will be trained in using advanced tools to diagnose, treat, and communicate with patients. In addition, improvements in virtual and augmented reality will provide students access to cutting edge learning tools. This will make their education more interactive and practical, potentially facilitating better understanding and knowledge retention.

AI in particular holds significant promise for medical students, training them to operate at a higher cognitive level and reducing time gathering data and information from multiple sources. According to Harvard Medical School educator Bernard Chang, MD, MMSc, "students ought to be able to move further along the developmental progression of reporter, interpreter, manager, and educator earlier in their training, reaching functional levels at which their cognitive talents will be most valuable in an AI-assisted clinical environment."

Future medical students will increasingly learn to work within and lead multidisciplinary teams. As the healthcare system shifts focus from treatment to prevention, medical students will pay closer attention to the social determinants of health and emphasize preventive care.

The COVID-19 pandemic has shown the importance of adaptability in healthcare. By virtue of having lived through the pandemic, medical students will show resilience and flexibility to changes in the healthcare environment, including changes in the way medicine is practiced and health systems achieve their goals. The whims of private equity and the business of medicine will become second-nature to them. With the rise of healthcare startups and new medical ventures, future medical students will learn entrepreneurial skills to innovate and improve the healthcare system. Clearly, tomorrow's medical students will be unlike any cohort of doctors in my time.

28.
What if Medical Students Were Taught the Way Musicians Learned How to Play?

Despite optimistic views expressed in the previous essay, medical education could still use a tune-up.

When I attended medical school in the 1970s, virtually all schools taught in a very traditional way: by lecturing on topics and subjects comprising individual courses. We were drilled in anatomy, biochemistry, pathology, pharmacology, and many other courses common to the biomedical sciences.

Traditional lecture-based learning was the norm until around the turn of the century, when there was a gradual transition to teaching medical students by a case-based method. Students began learning about diseases according to systems. Discussing clinical vignettes became central to the curriculum. Students were required to learn aspects of basic science courses that pertained to solving clinical problems and answering questions relevant to the case. The case-based method of learning evolved from problem-based learning and was touted for its deep learning.

There are other advantages of case-based learning too. It introduces clinical material early in the curriculum, links theory to practice through the application of knowledge to cases, and involves learning in small groups with common goals and objectives. Case-based learning mimics the real-world practice of medicine – especially working in teams – and learning from cases has been shown to be applicable to a wide variety of fields in healthcare as well as non-medical occupations.

Indeed, case-based teaching was the predominant learning method when I attended business school in the mid-1990s, nearly 15 years after graduating medical school. It was more popular (and appealing) than the lecture format because analyzing problems faced by real companies allowed students to generate their own insights and develop critical thinking and communication skills. Most MBA programs today are case-based – using Harvard Business School case packets – and require advanced reading and preparation as well as quality class participation, unlike my experience in medical school, which fostered post-hoc learning and the mere identification of correctly memorized answers from lectures.

The means by which medical students learn – sitting through lectures or studying cases in peer groups – bears a strong resemblance to learning to play the piano. Whether the piano is classified as a percussion or stringed instrument makes little difference in terms of how well it is played. The beauty of the instrument depends on the skill and competence of the piano player, which depends, in part, on how well the individual has been taught.

I was taught to play the piano the same way I was taught in medical school: the traditional way. I was taught through notation (reading and playing notes), the equivalent of taking courses and using them as educational building blocks. Practicing and rehearsing musical compositions was similar to memorizing medical facts and minutia; it was a repetitive process that lacked soul. I was force-fed classical music the same way I was mandated to take physiology, histology, and microbiology. I would have preferred playing the Beatles over Bach and Beethoven.

Studying medicine through case-based learning compares to the way children are taught to play the piano (and other instruments) via the Suzuki method – learning organically by ear rather than notation, and nourished by their parents and other "team" members. For Shinichi Suzuki, it was all about creating the right learning environment, and that placed aural learning at the heart of his method.

Listening skills are likewise essential when it comes to patient care. As William Osler, MD, famously said, "Just listen to your patient, he is telling you the diagnosis." I wonder if I would have been a better piano player – or doctor – had I been given lessons through the Suzuki method. I had a "Hard Day's Night" slogging through Bach and Beethoven sonatas. My preference for rock music, which could often be played by ear, was never taken into account by my music teachers.

Whether taught by the case-based method or traditional lectures, medical students must master a vast amount of information in the first 2 years of medical school. Students must acquire a certain level of knowledge so that when they enter their clinical rotations they are well-equipped to apply their knowledge in medical settings.

I find it interesting that the results of the U.S. Licensing Medical Examination (USMLE) Step 1 and 2 examinations for students enrolled in a problem-based versus traditional lecture-based curricula are roughly the same – both methods adequately prepare students for subsequent phases of their medical education and training. However, students clearly prefer learning from clinical cases and simulation as opposed to lectures. Osler recognized this over 100 years ago when he stated, "I wanted to be remembered for bringing the students out of the lecture hall and onto the wards."

There are pros and cons to traditional versus case-based learning approaches in medicine, just as there are pros and cons to different musical learning methods. I believe the best way to teach medical students is to pick from different methods of learning to ensure there is an adequate balance between theory and practice, instilling an appreciation for the history of medicine and the changing nature of diagnosis and treatment over time.

Although the piano has features of both percussion and stringed instruments, and has been classified in both categories, it is generally considered a combination of the two and is very unique in that respect.

Shouldn't the same hold true for the education of future doctors? Shouldn't medical students' learning preferences count, and shouldn't they be taught to integrate the art and science of medicine to be "in tune" with contemporary practice? Roll over Beethoven, tell Tchaikovsky the news.

29.
Is Your Medical Specialty Sustainable?

As you think about your current or intended specialty, can you visualize its future and how it will impact your practice and career satisfaction?

Medical students' selection of specialty is one of the most important choices they will ever make. But the decision of which medical specialty to enter can be difficult for many students. One of the difficulties lies in the fact that it is impossible for students to sample all their options while in medical school, let alone determine the ideal location to undertake training – assuming they match to their first choice.

Another reason choosing a specialty may be problematic is that medical fields change over time. My specialty of psychiatry, for example, was founded on the principles of psychotherapy – psychoanalysis in particular. But there have been significant declines in the provision of outpatient psychotherapy by U.S. psychiatrists over the past two decades. About half of psychiatrists do not incorporate psychotherapy into their practice, yet psychotherapy training continues to be required by psychiatric residency programs in order to maintain accreditation.

To choose a specialty, medical students need to think like Wayne Gretzky, a hockey player considered the greatest of all time. When asked how he managed to play so well and score so many goals, Gretzky said he skated to where he thought the puck would be, not where it was. By focusing on the future – where the puck is going to be – students can set themselves up to remain ahead of the curve and enjoy a specialty that will hold their interest for a lifetime. Choosing a specialty with staying power can also help them avoid burnout.

I'm no Wayne Gretzky, but I did tend to think like him when it came time to choose my specialty. I majored in psychology in college, and I always had an interest in the relationship between the brain and behavior. In my final year of medical school, I was well aware that the field of psychiatry was loosening its grip on psychotherapy and gravitating to an understanding of the biological basis of behavior. In hockey terms, my specialty choice was based on where I thought the puck was going to be, i.e., where the field of medicine was trending, particularly the practice of psychiatry.

There is an underlying assumption contained in Gretzky's quote: We can predict an outcome (where the puck is going to be) based on the detection of certain signals (where the puck is and what is happening at the time). To make sure I had a full view of the hockey arena, I consulted one of my mentors – a neurologist. I was equally as interested in neurology as I was in psychiatry, and I vacillated between the two disciplines.

I shared my dilemma with my mentor, and he replied, "Well, Art, if you want my opinion, one day psychiatry will become a subspecialty of neurology." The neurologist's forward-looking comment did not come true – at least not yet – but it is a fact that we now consider serious mental illnesses the equivalent of brain disorders, and both neurology and psychiatry have long been governed by the same Board of the American Board of Medical Specialties – namely, the American Board of Psychiatry and Neurology.

Today, the landscape of medicine looks vastly different than it did when I trained in the 1980s. Back then, artificial intelligence, telehealth, genetics and gene editing, and complementary and alternative medical practices were barely on the horizon, if at all. In my eventual area of specialization – pharmaceutical medicine – clinical trials were conducted at the site of the principal investigator, usually an academic medical center. Nowadays, decentralized clinical trials are the big rave. We are in the process of enabling clinical trials to be conducted at the home of subjects, much like making house calls. Decentralized trials aid in the recruitment and retention of subjects, increase the speed of the trial and diversity of subjects, and facilitate data collection.

Whether in practice or in industry, predicting how clinical scenarios will unfold is key to choosing where and how you may want to spend your working time. Unfortunately, critical areas of medicine like primary care practice are often the least satisfying specialties because advances in those fields tend to occur at a slow pace. On the other hand, specialties perceived to be dynamic and rapidly changing, and that offer a diversity of work, often provide the greatest personal fulfillment. You don't have to be a hockey superstar to know which way the wind blows. But you do have to do your homework and consider whether a given specialty is likely to innovate or remain stagnant.

As I previously mentioned, consulting with mentors – often academic faculty – can be helpful in arriving at a decision. Ironically, in my case, a physician who was not a specialist in my field influenced my decision. But just to be certain he had guided me in the right direction, I sought the advice of a well-known psychiatrist on staff at my medical school. I told him what the neurologist had said about how psychiatry is becoming absorbed by neurology. The psychiatrist paused and commented, "No, Art. The neurologist is wrong. Tell him one day psychiatry will become a subspecialty of toxicology."

I think they were both correct!

FOR RESIDENTS

30.
The Not-So-Private Lives of Young Physicians

Who would have imagined that faculty members would take to spying on residents' Facebook pages in an attempt to "normalize" their behavior? Why is it so important to scrutinize the social activities of dedicated young doctors? So many are sacrificing themselves in grueling residency programs. Doesn't that say enough about their character?

Apparently, several physicians affiliated with Boston University didn't think so. After collecting data from 2016 to 2018, findings on the prevalence of unprofessional social media content among young vascular surgeons were published in the *Journal of Vascular Surgery* (*JVS*). The journal's editorial board, representative of the white, male-dominated medical establishment, saw nothing wrong with the study. However, many readers disagreed, arguing that the findings were inherently biased and blatantly sexist.

In the wake of public backlash, two of the study authors tweeted identical apologies. In essence, they claimed their intent was empowerment but acknowledged that "the definition of professionalism is rapidly changing in medicine." The authors concluded: "We are sorry that we made the young surgeons feel targeted and that we were judgmental."

In their "research" paper, social snapshots of surgical trainees were harvested from Facebook, Twitter, and Instagram accounts. Approximately 25% of 235 doctors in the sample were identified as having content on social media that was either "clearly unprofessional" or "potentially unprofessional" (e.g., profanity; HIPAA violations; controversial religious, political, or social comments; inappropriate attire [e.g., women in bikinis!]; and depictions of drug paraphernalia or intoxication). The young surgeons were chided for their inappropriate behavior and warned to exercise caution when posting to public websites.

Articles of this sort have been published before, but in the wake of the #MeToo movement and other recent attempts to stamp out racism, sexism, and the disparagement of minority groups, the *JVS* study hit a raw nerve. Reactions to it were swift and overwhelmingly negative. Medical professionals flooded social media with pictures of themselves in bikinis with the hashtag #MedBikini, accompanied by sharp rebukes. The firestorm on Twitter (now X) forced the journal editors to retract the article in a statement posted, ironically, on Twitter.

Following the retraction, retweets and comments exploded, demonizing both the authors and the journal's editorial team. One physician wrote: "Maybe, instead of apologizing to those offended, you should apologize to the research subjects that you helped exploit. The trainees (in your own field!) that you have an obligation to mentor and support."

If one's interest in the private lives of young physicians is "empowerment," I can think of a half-dozen topics more worthy of medical attention and deserving of research – and none of them involve residents in swimsuits.

Improving the mental health of the next generation of physicians should be the real call to action. Surgical residents have an alarmingly high rate of burnout, and medical students begin to lose empathy as early as the third year of medical school, which is precisely when they are thrust into the clinical arena and begin interacting with patients. We cannot afford to let medical students and residents succumb to apathy and indifference as they are caring for patients.

Medical trainees are our frontline healthcare heroes. They demonstrated their heroics during the pandemic and afterward. But sometimes heroes need help, too. For all we know, social media provides a therapeutic outlet for their pain and woe. And it's worth noting that the *JVS* study did not conclude that doctors' social media profiles were harmful to patients.

It's time for academic faculty members to stop pimping new doctors and focus research efforts where they will actually be helpful. The voyeuristic behavior of medical school professors should be harshly condemned.

31.
PTSD After Medical Education

"Dear Art:

On Friday, June 11, 1982, members of the faculty convened to discuss the performance of the psychiatric residents during the last six (6) months. The following is a summation of their comments as they apply to your performance.

The faculty's reaction to your performance was uniformly excellent. There was some comment on your earlier fear of the psychotherapeutic role, but the consensus was that this has improved markedly and that you now have become more comfortable to the obvious pleasure of your faculty. There were comments about the diligence of your reading in the field and there were quotes such as "topnotch," "terrific," "a good teacher."

Art, the comments speak for themselves. We are delighted at your performance in the past year and consider you to be an outstanding resident. I am delighted with this report and look forward to your continuing in this direction in the next academic year.

Best wishes.
Sincerely yours,
[Name Withheld]
Professor and Chairman
Department of Psychiatry"

I received that letter over 40 years ago, at the end of a hellish second year of residency. Unknown to everyone except my spouse and psychiatrist,

I was recovering from the effects of "vicarious" – or "secondary" – trauma: the destructive emotional distress that results from an encounter with a traumatized and suffering patient who has suffered primary or direct trauma.

Only in my case I did not have a close encounter, at least not technically, because I never came to know the patient who traumatized me.

In the spring of 1981, toward the end of my first year of residency, I was "on call" and asked to give an opinion about a patient in the emergency department (ED) who was "hearing voices." The ED resident wanted my advice about his medication, but she said it was not necessary to come to the ED to evaluate him. After assuring me over the phone that the patient was not dangerous, I suggested she increase his haloperidol dose.

The patient was discharged, but he returned to the ED several hours later following a suicide attempt – the patient had jumped out the third-story window of his boarding home. He survived the fall but sustained significant orthopedic injuries.

I blamed myself for the incident, succumbing to the moral injury of violating my personal code of excellence. "I should have seen the patient," I thought. My injury was compounded by shame and guilt, as news of what had happened quickly circulated among the house staff. I became infamously associated with the "jumper." I slipped into a deep depression, barely able to function.

My midyear PGY-II evaluation (December 1981) was so bad that I was placed on probation. Clearly, I was not a rising star in the eyes of the faculty, some of whom had known me since I was a medical student. My fall from grace was cemented after one of the faculty members – the doctor who interviewed me in 1975 and recommended me for medical school admission – informed me there was no way to "sugarcoat" my abysmal performance.

Psychotherapy saved my life and allowed me to complete my residency, even regaining my star status as chief resident. But I was never able to overcome the "fear of the psychotherapeutic role" referenced in my chairman's letter. Every new patient encounter heightened my anxiety. What if they were suicidal? What if they were dangerous and harmed someone? I couldn't bear the thought of being responsible for someone's actions that might result in a fatal or near-fatal outcome and cause another stain on my record.

As a form of self-therapy, I published a "coming out" article about the incident in 2014 albeit decades after it occurred. I was humbled by the many physicians who responded to the article and shared similar experiences of vicarious traumatization.

An obstetrician-gynecologist wrote: "I, too, have a memorable patient I never saw when I was in training, and I continue to feel waves of shame and sadness over the outcome which might have been prevented if I had not gone back to sleep when the resident assured me that it was not necessary for me to see the patient."

A colleague confided that when he was a resident and moonlighting at a crisis center, he evaluated and discharged a man who went home and killed his partner. The homicide was covered by the local newspaper and television stations. My colleague escaped mention, but he was crushed by the ordeal, plagued by intrusive memories and disturbed sleep for months afterward – signs and symptoms typical of PTSD.

It is rarely appreciated that physicians who are exposed to traumatic events or trauma survivors can, themselves, become traumatized – approximately 10% to 20% develop PTSD. Surgeons and emergency medicine physicians tend to have higher rates of PTSD for obvious reasons: They treat a disproportionate number of traumatically injured patients. Psychiatrists and psychotherapists are susceptible because their patients discuss aversive details of traumatic experiences during therapy.

Physicians traumatized by unanticipated outcomes such as death; surgical complications; medical mistakes, errors, and misadventures; and malpractice litigation may also develop PTSD. These physicians often consider themselves "innocent bystanders" to trauma. Nevertheless, the emotional impact can be severe and lasting.

One physician who wrote to me recalled how he was traumatized by a malpractice lawsuit and further traumatized when his attorney pressured him to settle it. Failing to "get his day in court," where he was certain he would be vindicated, significantly contributed to his PTSD and "emotional inability to stay in practice."

It may be impossible for physicians to function normally again after exposure to trauma. The coronavirus pandemic was considered a traumatic stressor and is one of the top reasons so many physicians intend to leave practice long before retirement age. Many physicians feel they have been pushed to their limits, traumatized by a variety of practice-related stressors, not the least of which is working in dysfunctional health systems with high administrative burdens.

Whereas medical students frequently perceive themselves to be experiencing the symptoms of a disease they are studying, students are at real risk of suffering PTSD once they enter practice. My practice days ended fifteen years after my residency. I sought less stressful jobs in industry – pharmaceuticals and health insurance – and never looked back.

32.
Reconsidering the Art of Medicine

"Wherever the art of medicine is loved, there is also a love of humanity."
   – Hippocrates

The popular notion of post-traumatic stress disorder (PTSD) is that symptoms of the disorder, such as flashbacks, intrusive thoughts, and feeling on-guard, coincide with highly stressful and specific traumatic events, for example, wartime combat, physical violence, and natural disasters. In truth, affected individuals may be exposed directly or indirectly to the stressful event. Exposure to the stressor may involve actual or threatened death, serious injury, or sexual violence.

PTSD is usually not considered a result of medical training, but as I described in the preceding essay, it was in my case. Studies have shown that residents and physicians suffer a high rate of PTSD due to medical practice, whether or not they treat trauma patients or patients with life-threatening conditions. Apparently, the stress of practice alone is sufficient to cause symptoms characteristic of PTSD.

PTSD has also been diagnosed in professionals exposed to repeated or extreme aversive details of traumatic events in the course of health-related work. Examples include first responders collecting human remains, police officers repeatedly exposed to details of child abuse, and mental health therapists exposed to details of their patients' traumatic experiences.

James S. Kennedy, MD, formerly at Vanderbilt University Medical Center, stated, "The resulting feeling that physicians [with PTSD] ignore most is toxic shame…the belief that one is defective. Once in practice, patient care 'retriggers' the toxic fear, loneliness, pain, anger, and shame physicians experienced in training." Unlike healthy shame, in which the individual realizes they "did bad" and attempts to atone for it, toxic shame's message is, "I am bad," and it connotes a very different internal message. Shame is a key emotional reaction after experiences of trauma, and an emerging literature suggests that researchers have failed to recognize the influence of shame on post-trauma states.

PTSD is discussed in *What Doctors Feel: How Emotions Affect the Practice of Medicine* by Danielle Ofri, MD, PhD. Ofri, an associate professor of Medicine at New York University School of Medicine, describes the riveting story of Eva, a first-year pediatric resident who was traumatized when a senior resident instructed her to let a newborn infant die in her arms – in a supply closet of the hospital no less – because the infant was doomed to a quick death due to Potter syndrome.

Ofri commented, "Eva's residency was truly a traumatic experience in which survival was the mode of operation. And the PTSD that resulted was real…Certainly, in the breakneck pace of Eva's residency, there was barely a blip of acknowledgment for the wells of sadness that bloomed, day after day."

Ofri, herself, experienced long-lasting shame and humiliation after committing an error that nearly killed a patient. Exactly two weeks into the second year of her residency, Ofri mismanaged the insulin therapy of a patient in diabetic ketoacidosis. She was severely reprimanded by a senior resident in the presence of her intern. "I could almost feel myself dying away on the spot," Ofri remarks. "The details of my insulin error in the dingy Bellevue ER are crisply stored in the linings of my heart."

Ofri later felt compelled to write an entire book about medical mistakes: *When We Do Harm: A Doctor Confronts Medical Error*. The prompt for writing the book was not only Ofri's personal experience with medical error – "I've certainly made my share of them," she admits – but also because her editor at Beacon Press had inquired (in 2016) whether medical error was the third leading cause of death in the United States, as reported in the *British Medical Journal*.

The editor also asked Ofri whether it is true, according to the famous 1999 Institute of Medicine Report, *To Err is Human*, that nearly 100,000 people die in the U.S. due to medical misdeeds – the equivalent of about a jumbo jet's worth of patients crashing on U.S. soil every day? Ofri found that the number is probably smaller, maybe half the original estimate, but the impact of just one serious mistake can have a devastating effect on the career of any doctor.

In medical school, many of us are told to "get over" our insecurities and that we do not have time to grieve our mistakes. It is only through a "hidden curriculum" that we learn that not all patients can be saved or rescued. Over time, we realize the limits of our abilities. Recognition of what it really means to be a physician – the sense of power and powerlessness, of hope and helplessness – is both an attitude and a skill that must be acquired during training.

Still, it is legitimate to ask: Who provides physicians the necessary skills to cope with loss and despair? Who consoles us when our best turns out to be not good enough? Who teaches us how to deal with uncertainty inherent in medical practice? How do we rise above the scandal and embarrassment of making a mistake? And how do we overcome our fear of making mistakes?

I was unable to resolve these issues after my traumatic experience with the "jumper" – despite psychotherapy and support from my colleagues. Assurance that I was a good doctor was insufficient. Guidance from my mentors didn't sink in. Textbooks and self-help books seemed inadequate. I rejected advice to "get tough" with patients and, alternatively, to distance myself from them.

At least my residency director was able to open my eyes to the fact that psychiatry, like other specialties, has a mortality rate – from suicide and homicide. He said I could not predict the behavior of my patients with any more accuracy than could a lay person, much less that of a patient I had never seen. In fact, research has shown that psychiatric residents are not able to predict violent behavior in patients any better than chance.

Another faculty member pointed out that practice norms vary widely across the U.S. Neither evidence from clinical trials nor clinical observation can dictate action – nor inaction – in particular circumstances. The management decision for a single patient is complex, requiring a synthesis of incomplete and imperfect information and medical knowledge. "What makes you think," the psychiatrist probed, "this decision is made with any precision in the head of a sleep deprived resident?"

The psychiatrist's comment placated me and reminded me to be less hard on myself, to view practice protocols as guides to treatment, but to also realize how our emotions, prejudice, tolerance for risk, and personal knowledge of the patient guide our clinical judgment. Black-and-white approaches to patient management miss the shades of gray in between.

"We don't see things as they are, we see things as we are," noted Anaïs Nin. We learn how to obtain and accept outcomes – good or bad – even when care decisions are made with incomplete or flawed data and even in the haze of sleepiness. We allow our "sixth sense" to interact with formal approaches to the assessment and management of patients to alert us, instinctively, to potential danger and safety concerns, to channel our gut feelings and let us know how worried we should be when patients are not responding to conventional therapy. Science and artificial intelligence are of little help when we are out on a limb beyond the limits of our ingenuity and prowess. Only the art of medicine can guide us back to solid ground.

33.
Why Not Do Your Residency Where You Went to Medical School?

The pros and cons of training at your alma mater.

I read an interesting article written by an internal medicine physician who did his residency at the same institution he attended as a medical student. In his final year of residency, he received negative feedback from an attending who had known him as a student. The attending criticized the resident for showing less enthusiasm about patient care as compared to when he was a medical student.

The resident is now an attending physician himself at an academic medical center. Upon reflection, he acknowledges that he was grateful for the criticism he received as a resident, because the gut punch ultimately made him a better physician. Indeed, this physician has virtually all five-star ratings.

I, too, chose to stay at my medical school to do my residency training (in psychiatry). I had done a senior-year elective at the main teaching hospital, essentially functioning as a first-year resident. So, I knew what to expect if I stayed there for my residency. Besides, I felt comfortable "at home," and I had a positive experience that eliminated any concerns about choosing psychiatry as a specialty.

The faculty seemed genuinely interested in me. I had become acquainted with a few of them, beginning my freshman year and continuing into my senior year. But what I hadn't considered was the possibility that, since I was a "known quantity," training where I went to medical school could impose some risks. Specifically, my "honors" performance as a medical student could have raised the faculty's expectations of me, not unlike the aforementioned physician who was perceived to have been a failure for not becoming the doctor his attending thought he would become. Once people know you have a high-performance baseline, anything less might raise a red flag and invite unwelcome scrutiny leading to pressure to constantly overperform, fear of failure, and even burnout.

Still, whenever I counsel medical students about ranking residency programs, I always recommend they consider their own medical schools' programs (assuming they exist). Hopefully, the students have made a few inroads with faculty who are approachable and enjoy helping medical students succeed. I urge students to seek out attendings whom they admire and can tap as mentors during residency training.

Medical students must entertain a host of variables when it comes to deciding where they want to train. Once they've decided on a specialty, they have to weigh a variety of factors: geographic location, reputation of the program, work-life balance, the quality of the program director and other residents, and generally how good of a fit the program is.

Among U.S allopathic and osteopathic senior medical students, nearly half match to their first-choice residency programs. However, neither the National Resident Matching Program or the American Association of Medical Colleges routinely track the percentage of students who remain at their medical schools for training. The only information I found was in an online forum addressing whether the residency selection process might favor "same place" medical students, and there was no consensus on that topic.

To gain further insight into the advantages and disadvantages of staying at the same medical school to undertake residency, I asked a few colleagues for their opinions. The advantages were perceived to be basic familiarity with the hospital layout and function, infrastructure (including EMR), and faculty, as well as nurses and essential support staff. Several physicians believed that preexisting knowledge of the surrounding area and city would quickly enable students to establish a work-life balance and good relationships with patients. The workload distribution between medical students, residents, and fellows would already be known, allowing residents to plan their time more usefully.

The major disadvantage was a perception that by not leaving their home institution, medical students would not broaden their clinical experience, and they would have less opportunity for growth and future practice opportunities. A gastroenterologist stated, "If you train at the same system for med school, residency, and fellowship, you only get to see one narrow approach to medical care." An EM physician commented, "I've seen too many docs who went to residency and fellowship at the same program and they have no idea how the rest of the country practices." However, the fact remains that regardless of where physicians train, more than half will practice in their state of residency training.

Transitioning from medical school to residency can be daunting because it means applying theory to practice. It means more responsibility. It means being under a microscope. Knowing what to expect can help ease the fear and allow students to better prepare for the next few years. This is as good a reason as any to consider one's medical school as a place to train. In addition, if important groundwork has been laid in medical school, i.e., developing relationships with attending physicians, students are likely to succeed and even shine as residents at their alma maters.

FOR ATTENDINGS

34.
Avoid Burnout by Finding Your Fit in the Organization

Physicians who recognize the importance of cultural fit and attain it are more likely to be happy and productive.

Studies have shown a national burnout rate of more than 50% among physicians in practice. A 2018 survey conducted by Merritt-Hawkins revealed 78% of doctors sometimes, often, or always experience feelings of burnout. Physicians who transitioned from independent practice to employment in healthcare organizations reported higher rates of burnout, suggesting that working for large integrated health systems may not be an antidote for private practice-related stress.

As physicians seek employment, they should consider the "goodness of fit" between themselves and the organization. In the field of statistics, goodness of fit describes how well a model correlates with actual observations or values. Organizational psychologists borrowed the term to describe the compatibility of a person's temperament and skills with workplace requirements and environment. (Goodness of fit should not be confused with fitness for duty, which determines whether an individual can safely perform a defined job.)

The interaction between workplace variables and physician characteristics has a significant influence on the effects of work. The ultimate consequence of a poor fit is disillusionment, pessimism, burnout, and depression. Although major depressive disorder and burnout are clinically distinct entities, there is significant overlap in symptoms.

The cardinal manifestations of burnout syndrome – exhaustion, cynicism, and reduced personal accomplishment – threaten the health and well-being of physicians and, by extension, their patients. It is important for physicians to examine the goodness of fit prior to accepting a job offer in an organization lest they become victims of overwhelming work demands, prolonged stress, and other causes of burnout.

The impact work has on an individual's mental health and well-being is undeniable. It is said that at the height of his prominence nearly 100 years ago, Sigmund Freud was asked, "What is life all about?" He responded with 2 words: "Liebe und arbeit" (love and work). ("Play" was added years later.) Mental health benefits accrue when work is characterized by certain features common to good-fitting jobs.

Research has shown that individuals who fit in well with their organizations report higher levels of job commitment and satisfaction and less anxiety, depression, and substance use. In addition, working for a good-fitting organization leads to high individual productivity, low absenteeism, and few disability claims.

Although no single set of job characteristics is good or bad for everyone, and although job requirements may change over time, many conditions are important, perhaps prerequisite, for a good fit between physicians and organizations, and may diminish professional burnout:

1. **Type of Organization**. Organizations involved in mergers, acquisitions, downsizing, outsourcing, and other economic forces beyond their control put physicians' job security at risk. Continued exposure to market dynamics over which they have no control threatens physicians' job security and may lead to disillusionment, exhaustion, and a departure from clinical practice, as they grapple with the loss of autonomy and the prioritization of profit over patient care.

2. **Reporting Relationships**. Persistent conflict with a supervisor, a

board member, or a key stakeholder can shorten the tenure of employed physicians. New bosses who may be intent on replacing their direct reports with friends and former colleagues in a proverbial housecleaning may be difficult supervisors. Frontline leaders with poor leadership qualities have negative effects on the personal well-being and job satisfaction of the physicians they lead and burn them out over time.

3. **C-Suite Climate**. Physicians seeking employment as executives should gauge the temperament of non-physician executives with whom they will be working. Dissimilarities between physician executives and other leaders in the C-suite are the result of distinctive and different processes of training and professional socialization, as well as differences in psychological makeup, as reflected in Myers-Briggs personality types.

4. **Leadership**. All physicians are leaders at some level. They reach their fullest potential by becoming and remaining engaged while inspiring engagement and leadership in others. However, the differences mentioned in #3 (above) can lead to contrasting decision-making styles, communication preferences, and approaches to conflict resolution, which may create tension and a lack of opportunities for complementary perspectives in leadership dynamics.

5. **Communication**. Joseph Grenny, author of *Crucial Conversations* and the article "Speak Up or Burn Out," observes that physicians who engage more consistently and effectively in conversations that strengthen their social support systems and give them a greater sense of efficacy are less likely to burn out. Crucial conversations also breed powerful organizations toward which physicians gravitate.

6. **Career Development**. Physicians often cite stalled careers and lack of opportunity for advancement as reasons for burnout. Low morale and burnout often set in when physicians are not allowed to explore alternatives to traditional medical practice or are denied capital and other resources to

remain competitive and cutting edge in their specialty.

7. **Clear and Unambiguous** Roles. Studies have shown that role conflict and role ambiguity are significant factors in work stress among employees. When a clear path is not in sight, it is only natural for organizations to flounder and eventually fail for lack of focus and direction. Practicing under these conditions deflates physicians' morale and contributes to burnout.

8. **Goal Alignment**. Organizations and physicians need alignment of goals to create safe and high-quality care at lower cost. Mutually rewarding goals lead not only to business success, but also personal satisfaction. Goals that resonate with one's sense of purpose and meaning are likely to appeal to physicians, as are personal challenges and projects that lead to highly valued outcomes.

9. **Rewards and Retention**. Formalized physician reward and retention programs are growing in popularity. Rewards provide a competitive advantage in recruitment and help create camaraderie among the medical staff that is essential to preventing burnout. Retention programs have been shown to be particularly effective in reducing separation among early career physicians, considered a proxy for burnout.

10. **Social Engagement**. Collegial relationships are a major source of satisfaction for physicians. Although physicians relish clinical autonomy, they also appreciate a workplace where they can interact and network with peers, be recognized for good performance, and be included in management decisions.

11. **Culture**. Organizational culture encompasses values and behaviors that contribute to the unique social and psychological environment of a business. When physicians do not identify with the corporate culture, the result is a lack of trust, involvement, communication, and responsiveness to problem solving. The inability to practice within cultural norms is a significant driver of physician turnover, more so than inadequate compensation

and other sources of job dissatisfaction, such as regulatory and insurance requirements and electronic health record design and interoperability.

The takeaway is to do your homework and carefully assess the goodness of fit before accepting a job offer. Placing blind faith in a prospective employer may cut short your employment and increase the risk of burnout.

35.
Leaving a Toxic Workplace – And Preparing for One Less Toxic

View this transition as a chance to reassess your career path and make strategic choices for your future.

Many years ago, I left an organization that was extremely toxic. It was causing me to become depressed. During my exit interview, I was asked by a representative from human resources (HR) why I hadn't come forth earlier. She said she would have conducted a "climate assessment." A climate assessment takes the temperature of an organization and provides leadership with feedback by identifying areas of strength and those in need of improvement.

I was unaware such a mechanism was available to me. Instead, I clung to my job despite its toxic effects. I later learned from a physician who had previously held the same position that he, too, became clinically depressed. The source of our distress was our boss, whom we both felt had a severe personality disorder. Toxic bosses harm employees in countless ways, and estimates suggest abusive supervisors cost organizations millions in lost productivity, employee turnover, and litigation each year.

In rare instances, the behaviors of toxic leaders can "trickle down" to affect the actions of employees at lower organizational levels, resulting in abused supervisors who abuse their own subordinates, much like the cycle of abuse seen in families. However, research shows that people who disidentify with their toxic boss are less likely to adopt bad behavior – especially when the person has high integrity and morals.

My upfront advice is to learn how to read the tea leaves and quickly depart any company that is making you sick. It took more than 100 doctors and faculty members at the University of Virginia (UVA) School of Medicine and health system to highlight the toxic working conditions there. They signed a no-confidence letter (dated September 5, 2024) against two physician administrators. The letter included allegations over concerns about patient safety, such as quality of new doctor hires; fear of retaliation against those who raise concerns about patient safety, capacity constraints, and moral distress; excessive spending on C-suite executives amid staffing shortages; and failure to be forthcoming on significant financial matters. The letter also mentioned that the environment fostered by the physician administrators has contributed "to an ongoing exodus of experience and expertise at all levels."

Such displays of unison among faculty are rare. It is more typical of physicians to hold on to toxic jobs or work for toxic bosses to the point where it is affecting their health. This is usually due to a combination of financial, professional, and psychological factors. Financially, the significant investment in medical education and training, coupled with the high costs of student loans, can make the prospect of leaving a steady job daunting.

Professionally, physicians may fear damaging their reputation or career trajectory by leaving a position prematurely, especially in a field where relationships and networks are crucial. Additionally, the deeply ingrained culture of resilience and dedication in medicine can lead physicians to endure adverse conditions, believing it's their duty to persevere for the sake of their patients. Furthermore, toxic leaders may manipulate or undermine physicians' confidence, making them feel trapped or incapable of finding better opportunities.

Lastly, the scarcity of job openings in certain specialties or geographic locations can limit options, compelling physicians to stay in less-than-ideal work environments. These intertwined factors create a complex scenario where physicians might remain in toxic settings despite the personal and professional toll it takes on them.

Assuming you find your situation intolerable, deciding to move on is often essential for both personal and professional well-being. It's important to start by reflecting on the specific aspects of the environment that are toxic and how they impact you. This self-awareness will be invaluable in avoiding similar situations in the future and in understanding what you truly need in your next role.

As you plan your exit, consider the timing of your departure carefully. Ensure that you have another opportunity lined up or sufficient savings if you plan to take a break. Review your employment contract to understand the notice period and any other obligations you might have. Discreetly reach out to your professional network to explore new opportunities, and take the time to update your resume and LinkedIn profile with your latest accomplishments and skills. When applying for new positions, focus on roles and organizations that align with your career goals and personal values, as I discussed in the previous essay.

Throughout this process, it's crucial to maintain professionalism. When drafting your resignation letter, keep it concise and positive, avoiding any mention of negative experiences. If you are offered an exit interview, provide constructive feedback but be careful not to burn bridges. This approach will help preserve your professional relationships and reputation.

Taking care of your mental and physical health is also important during this transition. Engage in activities that reduce stress, such as exercise, meditation, or pursuing hobbies (see essay 39). Don't hesitate to lean on friends, family, or a mentor for support as you navigate this change. Finally, reflect on what you've learned from this experience and how it can guide your future career decisions. Keep a positive outlook and focus on the opportunities that lie ahead, knowing that you are taking proactive steps toward a more fulfilling work life.

36.
Does Ageism Lurk Behind Mandatory Retirement?

"The young man knows the rules, but the old man knows the exceptions."
– Oliver Wendell Holmes

A good friend and colleague – the chairman of a psychiatry department – notified people he was retiring. In a department newsletter, he wrote, "I sent out a letter to the alumni and adjunct faculty that I will retire on June 30 [2021]. I had decided five years ago that when I reached a certain age, I was going to retire. Such decisions have multiple determinants and are made with ambivalent feelings."

My friend was on the faculty for 20 years and chairman for half that time. He further wrote, "It has been a wonderful journey. Watching many residents and faculty become outstanding clinicians, educators, and researchers has been an honor and joy. These wonderful relationships are part of the tapestry of my memory and will always remind me of my years at [the medical school]. I am leaving a vibrant, energetic, and young faculty."

"Why retire?" I thought. It didn't make sense that my friend would impose an age limit on himself to retire when he was 70 and cognitively intact. Sometime later I discovered that he had become embroiled in conflict with the university, and his departure had nothing to do with his age, competence, or views about his age.

Yet I know there are times when aging physicians begin to show signs of dementia and are singled out for neuropsychological evaluations. Similarly, some surgeons seem physically unfit to operate and are subjected to ophthalmological and neurological testing. In fact, this topic – the competency of older physicians to practice medicine – has become a raging controversy.

The issue concerns whether physicians should be forced to retire at a certain age like other professionals – judges, FBI agents, commercial pilots, air traffic controllers, military officers, national park rangers, and others. During her short-lived 2024 presidential campaign, former South Carolina Governor Nikki Haley called for mandatory competency tests for politicians older than 75. "In the America I see, the permanent politician will finally retire," Haley said – except most older voters balked at her idea and instead elected a 78-year-old president (Donald J. Trump).

The argument for mandatory retirement almost always centers on public safety. Older ("permanent") physicians are believed to threaten patients' safety because aging impacts not only cognition but also vision, hearing, dexterity, stamina and judgment. A 2005 article in the *Annals of Internal Medicine* kicked off a firestorm when the authors reviewed 62 studies and found that more than half (52%) showed a decline in patient outcomes with advanced practitioner age (only one study showed improvement).

A 2017 study in the *British Medical Journal* offered further proof that aging results in errors and poorer quality care. Among hospitalists in charge of Medicare patients, older physicians had higher 30-day mortality rates than those cared for by younger physicians, despite similar patient characteristics. The only variable that resulted in comparable mortality rates was high patient volume, in which case, young or old, it didn't make a difference in patient mortality.

However, a 2021 analysis of 52 studies found quite the opposite, i.e., physicians' clinical experience (a proxy for age) and quality tended to be positively correlated. Moreover, in a study of surgeons, age was not an important predictor of operative risk, including mortality, for most procedures. In yet another study, residents, and attendings were judged to be equal in their safety outcomes. A subsequent study of emergency medicine physicians found that older physicians fared better than younger ones in terms of committing fewer errors, prompting some to argue that training resources should be directed toward novice physicians instead of elderly ones.

Overall, the literature on this subject is complicated and conflicting, with marked variation in results and divided opinions about implementing mandatory competency testing or retirement for physicians, usually beginning at age 70.

Ageism is one significant factor that clouds findings and interpretations – the elephant in the room. The term "ageism" was coined in 1968 by psychiatrist Robert N. Butler (1927-2010), who became the first director of the National Institute on Aging. Butler, a fierce defender against discrimination and stereotypes of the elderly, compared ageism to racism, claiming it was "prejudice by one age group toward other age groups." (Butler did not discuss "reverse ageism" coming from older workers toward younger professionals.)

In one of his seminal papers, "Age-Ism: Another Form of Bigotry," Butler wrote: "Ageism reflects a deep-seated uneasiness on the part of the young and middle-aged – a personal revulsion to and distaste for growing old, disease, disability; fear of powerlessness, 'usefulness,' and death." I do not doubt that much of the controversy surrounding the mandatory retirement of physicians is rooted in ageism.

Nowhere is this more evident than in institutions embarking on late-career practitioner screening programs, notably Yale New Haven Hospital, which is tied up in litigation with the U.S. Equal Employment Opportunity Commission over attempts to evaluate physicians simply because they are old. At Yale and other institutions, it is quite possible that policies such as Yale's "Late Career Practitioner Policy" may reflect ageist attitudes rather than genuine concerns about patient safety, and that implicit (unconscious) bias may be at work – a type of microaggression toward the elderly.

A 2022 study from Switzerland bears this out. There was a tendency among 234 human resource (HR) employees to see themselves as less biased than their HR peers or to be able to identify more cognitive biases in others than in themselves in their hiring decisions. The presence of a biased "blind spot" was thus confirmed. Furthermore, male HR employees showed a greater bias blind spot than female HR employees.

Age bias is one of the most common types of discrimination in the workplace today. This is very concerning for physicians, given that approximately 47% of active physicians in the U.S. in 2021 were 55 or older, and some plan to practice until they are in their 70s or 80s. An age mandate to retire will deplete the physician workforce and wreak havoc on a system already facing dire shortages.

For sure, there are physicians advancing in age who should be removed from the workforce. There are also early-career physicians who should not be allowed to practice. Assessing physician competencies and capabilities based on identities like age and other demographics is only a hop-skip-and-jump away from using other factors like illness, gender, or race as cause for discriminatory policies disguised as "patient safety."

The solution is to target the performance of individual physicians when their abilities are in question rather than target an entire class of physicians and begin collecting normative data for various age groups to prevent judgments from being made in isolation.

The AMA Principles of Medical Ethics also propose a way to solve the conundrum of mandatory retirement. It recognizes that physicians have a duty to monitor the quality of care they deliver as individual practitioners, e.g., through personal case review and critical self-reflection, peer review, and the use of other quality improvement tools. Physicians are responsible for maintaining their health and wellness. When practice issues arise, take measures to mitigate them, seek appropriate help as necessary and engage in an honest self-assessment of their ability to continue practicing.

For example, Richard Rothman, MD (1936-2018), was one of the nation's most prominent and respected orthopedic surgeons. He was still doing surgery at age 80. However, he had his vision checked regularly and asked a senior partner to monitor the quality of his work for a day (he did fine). Rothman may have been a role model for the AMA, but how often can physicians be expected to follow his lead?

37.
Are Physicians with MBAs Traitors to Health Care?

Contrary to concerns that dual-degree physicians are disinterested in clinical care, the vast majority leverage their new perspectives and skills to improve healthcare delivery.

I have an MD degree and an MBA degree. I earned my medical degree in 1980 and my business degree in 1996. I wrote the first definitive textbook about physicians with dual degrees (MD-DO/MBA). Subsequently, I've written many papers on the topic, and I maintain articles and news clippings in several file folders each 3 to 4 inches thick. I keep track of current trends. I encourage medical students and early career physicians to apply to business school if they have a genuine interest in the business and management aspects of medical practice.

However, the topic of dual-degree physicians sometimes unnerves me. I am sensitive to unkind remarks made about physicians with MD (or DO) and MBA degrees. After I published an op-ed about "faking" my way through medical school, a physician responded, "I believe that the author who has by his name, MD and MBA, suggests he likely never was made for medicine." What a sanctimonious doctor!

Physicians have been seeking MBA degrees for decades. Both the number of executive MBA programs and the number of MD/MBA programs offered by medical schools has steadily increased, as has the number of physicians receiving MBA degrees from these programs. The trend first became newsworthy in 1994, when the *Wall Street Journal* published an article with the title "A New Breed of M.D.s Add M.B.A. to Vitae," written by George Anders.

Anders appeared to have penned the piece believing that, based on his interview sources, adding an MBA degree to one's MD degree was a way to enhance physicians' marketability and allow them to "pivot quickly… between the world of stethoscopes and the world of spreadsheets." An MBA degree was viewed as a "ticket to open doors" and put doctors on a fast-track for hospital leadership positions. Physicians' motivation for obtaining MBA degrees today remains basically the same as it did 30 years ago – to learn more about the business of healthcare and prepare them for taking on additional administrative responsibilities.

Several years after the *Wall Street Journal* article was published, the late distinguished physician Leonard Laster, MD, wrote the book *Life After Medical School*. In the book, Laster categorized and described five basic career pathways in medicine: primary care; surgery; psychiatry; disciplines removed from ongoing patient care (anesthesiology, pathology, radiology and nuclear medicine) and areas that bear little if any relationship to medical practice – for example, management and politics.

Further thoughts about the fifth career pathway – pursuits distanced from clinical medicine – led Laster to write a scathing article in 1998 in the now defunct *American Medical News*, which served as the official publication of the American Medical Association. The article was titled: "Physicians with MBAs? Not my doctor!" Laster opined that physicians cannot – and should not – serve two masters, concluding: "I will not allow my family members to be guinea pigs for testing whether these professional polarities [medicine and business] can be successfully used. I say let businessmen be businessmen and pursue profits, and let doctors be doctors and care for patients."

Laster's op-ed enraged readers and generated more letters to the editor than any article previously published in *American Medical News*. Obstetrician/gynecologist G.V. Raghu, MD, wrote a letter expressing the sentiments of many physicians who responded to Laster's commentary. Raghu wrote: "It is amazing that Leonard Laster, MD...looks at MBA training as an antithesis of medical values. Does he prefer nonphysician MBAs to be making the management, cost-cutting and quality management decisions?" Dr. Raghu – and many physicians since 1998 – have thoughtfully made the case that dual-degree physicians would be a positive influence on how care is delivered.

The great debate about physicians with MBAs thus became entrenched in articles and letters, with definitive data lacking to answer the question whether an MBA degree adds real value for physicians or forces them to live by two incompatible creeds. In the continued absence of such data and notwithstanding the perceived value of an MBA degree including larger salaries for dual-degree physicians, the debate still rages.

Many academicians consider dual-degree physicians traitors to the medical profession despite research showing that business skills do not, in fact, lower practice competencies or draw students away from medicine. I've had to counsel several entrepreneurial medical school applicants and advise them to curb their enthusiasm about business school lest the interviewer would reject them outright. I'm not convinced there is ever a good time for medical students and residents to declare their interest in business school. For various reasons, they may benefit by waiting until after residency to pursue an MBA degree.

Fortunately, a few level-headed and well-respected academicians have chimed in to even the debate. One, in particular, is my good friend and colleague David Nash, MD, MBA, founder and dean emeritus of the Jefferson College of Population Health in Philadelphia, Pennsylvania. In 1986, Nash and two colleagues anticipated the need for management-trained physicians to lead the "medical industrial complex." In their article published in *The New England Journal of Medicine*, they did not specify the importance of a business degree, but they argued that physicians needed additional training in management theory, educated perhaps through professional organizations (business school was not a popular option at that time).

In 1999, Thomas Bodenheimer, MD and Lawrence Casalino, MD, PhD wrote a two-part article also in *The New England Journal of Medicine* apparently legitimizing the role of "[physician] executives with white coats." They described various roles and responsibilities of HMO medical directors. But in doing so, they continued the debate started by Laster. Bodenheimer and Casalino wrote: "The two opposing views reflect inherent conflicts in the role of medical directors – between the desires of patients and physicians, on the one hand, and the financial profit or survival of the organization, on the other, and between the unlimited demands of individual patients and the limited resources of society." Simply put, business-minded physicians are – and always will be – stuck between medicine and management.

Diana Chapman Walsh, president emeritus of Wellesley College, published her PhD thesis as a book about corporate physicians. She offers a management lesson not taught in medical or business school – one that needs to be learned through experience and deep personal reflection: physicians must learn how to manage the tension that exists between their obligations as doctors and their role as part of management. This applies equally to physicians working for organizations and those who are self-employed. Unless this underlying conflict is appropriately handled, physicians risk harm to their patients and reputations, and they may remain unpopular with their colleagues.

38.
Let's Not Discourage Our Children from Becoming Doctors

Physicians who are parents and rally against medical careers for their children truly represent the "great resignation" in medicine.

By now, most of us are familiar with the term the "Great Resignation" – the tidal wave of people quitting their jobs, in the U.S. and around the world. The Great Resignation began primarily in response to the coronavirus pandemic, but additional factors have sustained it. Health care is the second largest sector hit by the Great Resignation (food services is number one).

The term "Great Resignation" was coined by organizational psychologist Anthony Klotz, PhD, MBA, an associate professor of management at May Business School at Texas A&M University. Klotz explains, "From organizational research, we know that when human beings come into contact with death and illness in their lives, it causes them to take a step back and ask existential questions like what gives me purpose and happiness in life, and does that match up with how I'm spending my [time] right now? So, in many cases, those reflections will lead to life pivots."

Perhaps the most disturbing trend of the Great Resignation is the long-term implications. In order for resignations to be filled – especially doctors' jobs – we should be encouraging our children to consider a career in medicine, along with other, more immediate measures aimed at boosting staffing levels.

Stimulating an interest in the field of medicine is a good long-term strategy to replenish healthcare jobs. Not uncommonly, one or both parents who are – or were – physicians plant the seed to become a doctor early in their children's lives. The seedlings are cultivated with loving care until they germinate into premedical students, accepted into medical school on their own merit or as "legacy" students. In either case, some individuals would not have become doctors if it weren't for encouragement from their parents and high praise lavished upon the medical profession.

However, in a time where burnout and exhaustion are widespread, many physicians debate whether or not they would advise their children to follow in their footsteps. Even Hippocrates was uncertain about the rewards of a career in medicine. "The life so short, the craft so long to learn," he famously said. The crux of the matter is often viewed in terms of a tradeoff between the time invested to become a doctor and the return on investment – not only the financial return, but especially the personal gratification of practicing medicine.

A poll conducted by Doximity is quite revealing. Of 7950 physicians who responded to an online survey in 2023, 63% said they would probably or definitely not want their children to work in medicine. Overall, physicians were 2% less likely to want their children to pursue medicine compared with previous Doximity poll results. Although some doctors continue to invoke the "medicine is a calling" argument, fewer are inclined to see it that way.

The most common reasons physicians rally against medicine as a profession for their children are those we've been reading about for the past decade: heavy caseloads, long hours, loss of autonomy, third party intrusions, toxic work cultures, and negative impacts on personal relationships. One family medicine physician asked: "Why make them [our children] suffer what we are suffering in this horrible situation created by EHRs, insurers, burocrats [sic], and so on and so forth?"

To be sure, a vocal minority did advocate for the profession. "I would be so proud to see my children continuing in this noble profession," a telemedicine physician commented. A neurosurgeon incredulously asked, "What can be more satisfying than saving lives?" A geriatrician said, "It's a great joy for me to see the likes of [my daughter] and her friends entering our still sacred profession and I hold out hope that they can smooth the rough edges."

That sentiment was echoed by many physicians who said that medicine was a worthwhile profession, describing it as a "privilege," but only if their children have the "passion" and "desire" to enter practice. That makes me wonder, how much influence do we have over our children's career choices? While we cannot decide their future, we can encourage an interest in STEM and introduce them to the field of medicine through career fairs and job shadowing. But at the end of the day, most children will follow their hearts and not our wishes or dreams.

Three of my 4 adult children are healthcare practitioners. They made their own career decisions, and I encouraged and supported them. I didn't try to steer any of them into medicine, although I've always believed it was a great profession and told them so.

I'm afraid, however, that not enough physicians share my conviction. I'm saddened by surveys that indicate that nearly half of physicians would not choose medicine again for themselves. The moniker the "Great Resignation" can also be applied to those among us who hesitate to speak proudly of our profession and promote medicine as an honorable career – one worthy to serve the suffering, to paraphrase William Root, MD – and who fail to inspire promising students to choose medicine as a career.

The story I've repeatedly told my children (and others) comes from *The Field of Dreams*, the scene where Ray Kinsella (Kevin Costner) tries to persuade Dr. Archibald ("Moonlight") Graham (Burt Lancaster) to travel back in time to experience a once in a lifetime opportunity: a chance to bat in the major leagues. Dr. Graham refuses to go with Ray, and Ray exclaims: "It would kill some men to get so close to their dream and not touch it. God, they'd consider it a tragedy." To which Dr. Graham replies, "Son, if I'd only gotten to be a doctor for 5 minutes … now that would have been a tragedy."

FOR EVERYONE

39.
Are Your Hobbies Connected to Your Specialty?

The issue of professional identity is complex, especially for those of us who have significant interests outside of medicine. Each activity informs the other, and being able to fluidly go between them is a mark of flexibility that can only enhance, not detract from, our role as a doctor.

Throughout my career I have met doctors with some of the most interesting hobbies – car collectors, wine makers, coffee roasters, and many others. I've often wondered whether physicians who have utilized their specialized skills in the practice of medicine have parlayed those skills into hobbies. In other words, is there a connection between physicians' hobbies and their medical specialty? My take is that doctors' hobbies and their specialty choices are often inextricably linked.

The COVID-19 pandemic drew considerable attention to the importance of having a hobby. Physicians under prolonged stress needed outside activities to decompress from hard-fought battles lost and won on the COVID front lines. It's impossible to say whether having a hobby would have mitigated the exodus of physicians after COVID and since then, but the importance of having a hobby has been shown to be crucial in achieving relaxation and work-life balance, as well as coping with anxiety, depression, and traumatic medical experiences.

My son-in-law, for example, is a medical resident and an avid gardener. Gardening has allowed him to unwind from the pressure of residency (emergency medicine), while simultaneously parenting two young children. He feels that gardening has made him a better clinician by teaching him to be patient, learning from failure, and accepting death. Most importantly, gardening has taught my son-in-law concepts related to preventive medicine.

He wrote a thoughtful "Op-Med" in Doximity (August 18, 2021) in which he stated "Any gardener knows the importance of their soil's composition. You need to have the right amounts of organic matter, nutrients, minerals, fungi, and bacteria to give your plants the best foundation to grow ... The garden has reminded me that in order to help our patients grow and maintain their health for longer periods of time, we must grant them solid ground beneath their feet and a clinician who can help them when needed."

One of my most influential and admired professors (emeritus) at my medical school is infectious disease expert Bennett Lorber, MD, a professional painter. Lorber was raised in a family that valued art and music – his cousin is the accomplished jazz keyboardist and Grammy award winner Jeff Lorber – and Lorber has painted since early childhood. He also emphasized the importance of having a hobby as a doctor. "Doing something that is important to you, makes you happy, and keeps you sane is just as important as what you do as a doctor ... To best take care of patients, you have to first take care of yourself ... I am a doctor and a painter. Painting for me is not a hobby, but rather a calling equal to my calling to medicine," he said.

Some incredibly talented physicians have found their calling outside of medicine and have left the profession altogether. But the overwhelming majority are satisfied to straddle the fence, like psychiatrist and world-renowned jazz pianist Denny Zeitlin, MD, who maintains a private psychotherapy practice when not recording or touring.

On his website, Zeitlin discusses striking similarities between his two vocations: "The psychotherapeutic journey has commonalities with improvising music, which, as a jazz pianist and composer, has been another major passion. Empathy and communication are paramount in both, and I believe my most creative level of psychotherapy and musical expression occurs when I am able to trust that I will be able to bring to bear everything I have studied and learned while simultaneously allowing myself to be so immersed in the activity that I become 'one' with it – to merge with the music, the musicians, or the patient and his psychological life. I've been fascinated with the nature and challenges of this merger state ... The cross-pollination of music and psychiatry has greatly aided me in both fields."

Success notwithstanding, Zeitlin is quick to add that his musical activities have always remained subordinate to his primary responsibilities to patients and trainees (he teaches at the University of California, San Francisco).

The same holds true for general surgeon and kiln-formed glass artist Steven Immerman, MD, who specializes in treatment for pilonidal disease. "Though I was extremely busy, I knew I needed a creative outlet," he said. "I found I really missed having a hobby in which I could use my hands. I was a surgeon at work, but even at play, I needed to work with my hands."

Once when Immerman attended a workshop and proposed a project – a block of colored glass with a window through which viewers could observe the contents inside – the instructor remarked, "Well, of course. You're a surgeon. You make little openings in people and you look inside."

Immerman has since observed similar parallels between people's choice of work and their extracurricular activities. Perhaps the most profound parallel can be seen in his own practice, because both surgical and artistic outcomes entail a period of waiting and uncertainty. "They both have a period of time when the process is seemingly out of my control," he said. "For surgery, it is the patient's healing process; for kiln-formed glass, it is the time it is in the kiln. Then, hopefully, there is the joy of seeing the finished product in both endeavors." Immerman also cited the example of a pathologist friend who enjoys astronomy in his spare time. "Both activities consist of looking through a lens and making order out of chaos," he observed.

I have searched for correlations in my own career, as an established psychiatrist and an amateur musician who plays piano and collects rock and roll live music recordings. As best I can determine, with psychotherapy as my currency, the flow of the therapeutic conversation (the melody), combined with the spoken word of the patient (the lyrics), unites my practice with my hobby.

The relationship between work and hobbies need not be esoteric. For example, Christos Ballas, MD, a very busy ob/gyn, trains and competes in triathlons. He noted, "My hobby is like my career, a big grind, but a lot healthier than going to work. I train and do endurance events, so when not working I'm swimming, running, or biking and thankful that at 61 I can still do it and practice full scope ob/gyn."

I invited physicians blogging on Doximity to share their views about the similarities between their hobbies and medical specialties. A plastic surgeon stated that he makes large-scale production model cars. "Maybe my hobby makes me a different kind of 'plastic' surgeon," he surmised. Emergency medicine physician and author Jeffrey Wade, MD, commented, "Stories are a way I receive the world as a big reader and how I report it back. Writing stories from my life has almost been like psychotherapy and gives me individual stories or books to hand out to people who seem like they could benefit from it."

A retired ER trauma physician stated that he builds and shoots black powder Buffalo rifles from the 1800s and percussion muskets and flintlocks from the 1700s. What a curious hobby, I thought, for a physician who has probably treated hundreds, if not thousands, of gunshot victims during his career.

Physicians who are accomplished in their specialties and hobbies usually thrive on the interplay between them. It makes sense that our hobbies reveal a great deal about our passions and the activities that sustain us. Although our hobbies may not always align with our work, it's possible that the more it does, the higher our level of job satisfaction.

In fact, when graduating medical students were asked to rank the most important factors that influenced their specialty choice, "fit with personality, interests, and skills" consistently ranked the highest, behind specialty content, work-life balance, length of residency, and income expectations. The factors motivating physicians to pursue certain career pathways may be the very same factors leading them to choose lifelong hobbies.

40.
The Impact of Imposter Syndrome on Physicians' Practice and Leadership Development

Physicians with imposter syndrome have significant difficulty suppressing feelings of inadequacy – feelings that often persist throughout their career.

The impostor phenomenon (IP), also known as imposter syndrome (IS), was first described in 1978 by psychologists Pauline Rose Clance and Suzanne Imes. It was defined as an internal experience of intellectual phoniness in high-achieving women who seemed to be unable to internalize and accept their success. These women believed each new task would expose them as frauds, and they found countless ways to discredit their accomplishments despite receiving positive feedback and high accolades from their mentors and peers.

IS has since been observed in many high-stakes professions including business, law and medicine. Doctors who exhibit IS display symptoms common to other professionals such as anxiety, depression, shame, and burnout. In rare instances, suicide may result.

Symptoms of IS stem primarily from prolonged isolation and stress and an inability to meet self-imposed standards of achievement in individuals typically characterized as perfectionists and "type A" personalities, which encompasses most medical professionals. It is important to note, however, that IS does not necessarily equate with low self-esteem or a lack of self-confidence. The dominant theme is chronic self-doubt and a sense of intellectual fraud that override any feelings of success or evidence of competence.

Prevalence rates of IS in medical professionals vary widely, encompassing 22% to 60% or more of physicians and physicians in training. The sheer prevalence was emphasized by a surgeon who commented, "I'd like to meet someone who HASN'T experienced imposter syndrome." In this vein, IS has been compared to burnout syndrome: both constitute "a problem to be confronted at the organizational level with serious engagement from leadership and investment in both cultural transformation and policy change."

A 2016 study found that almost a quarter of male medical students and nearly half of female students experienced IS. Approximately one-third to one-half of medical residents have been identified as having IS. Even seasoned clinicians, those at advanced stages in their career, have questioned the validity of their achievements and reported feelings of imposture. Some believed they had "risen to the level of their incompetence," suggesting that past accolades could not buffer their insecurities, which they rarely shared with colleagues.

There is a robust literature that describes the negative association between IS and job satisfaction and performance leading to meaningful setbacks in the careers of some individuals and forcing others to abandon their profession altogether. Manifestations of IS that may adversely impact physicians and aspiring physician leaders include a lack of courage to take on new professional challenges, accept new assignments and projects, and learn new skills.

The symptoms of IS may be transient, but without treatment, IS is likely to be chronic with acute exacerbations of and anxiety and self-doubt when novel challenges and situations arise. It is not uncommon for IS symptoms to be present during medical training or when starting one's career, although some physicians may harbor life-long doubts about their abilities and believe it's only a matter of time before they're "found out."

Physicians plagued by IS, particularly those with misplaced self-doubt who are unable to accurately assess their skills and abilities and are unreceptive to corrective feedback, tend to become less motivated and productive over time. They display self-handicapping behaviors such as procrastination and perfectionism. It's been said that perfection is the enemy of success, while a growth mindset is its greatest friend. Unfortunately, victims of IS are robbed of their growth potential.

Trainees and physicians with IS may feel unprepared for the next stage of their careers or future job prospects. They may avoid prominent leadership opportunities and fail to reach their full potential because the additional responsibility and visibility that comes with a leadership role intensifies their performance anxiety. In short, physicians with IS may be passed over for leadership positions, use flawed logic to exclude themselves from consideration, or fail as physician leaders.

When a physician feels like a phony, it can create a ripple effect. A physician's drive to pursue prestigious residencies, fellowships or promotions may be thwarted by an inner voice that tells them they're not qualified and would not be selected. Doctors who believe they are imposters may behave in such a way as to cut short their potential to become physician leaders. IS could be the reason why some promising physicians appear to have unfulfilled talent and are "held back" in their careers.

IS doesn't affect a person's ability to shoot, but it affects where they aim. This means that from a career perspective, despite significant achievements, physicians with imposter syndrome often aim low in order to limit their visibility lest others detect their (imagined) fraudulence. Their careers become truncated by mental paradigms that dictate "I am a failure," "I am a fake," and "I am not successful." In the mind of an imposter, success is the result of chance, and good luck will surely run out. Imposters pass up significant career opportunities because they are convinced they won't be able to do better elsewhere.

Recognizing that many trainees and newly minted attendings feel like imposters, my advice to them is as follows:

- Imposter syndrome is a name only. Don't let it derail you from your goals and aspirations.
- Realize that feelings of inadequacy are normal and ubiquitous among your peers. Don't be imprisoned by the fear of making mistakes – everybody makes them.
- Remember that the biggest misconception about Abraham Lincoln is that he was perfect. However, Lincoln is often cited as someone who likely experienced imposter syndrome, essentially feeling like he wasn't qualified for the role of President despite his accomplishments.
- Cognitive distortions of your abilities and achievements are just that – distortions, which are correctable, either through self-reflection, mentorship, professional coaching, or cognitive behavioral techniques to reframe negative thought patterns.
- You are not a fraud. You haven't gotten this far by accident. You have what it takes to be an excellent clinician and leader.

41.
Reflections on Human Suffering

Friedrich Nietzsche said, "He who has a why to live for can bear almost any how." *The operative word is "almost."*

I was in my upstairs home office when I heard the doorbell ring. I ran downstairs to open the door, unable to see through the opaque window who was on the other side. I opened the door and there stood an elderly Black man and woman, well dressed, with leaflets and literature. I immediately recognized that this was an unsolicited proselytization.

"Can I help you," I inquired? The woman handed me a pamphlet and asked, "Do you believe that human suffering will end?" I glanced at the pamphlet but not really searching for the answer.

"I'm tied up at the moment ma'am, but 'no,' I do not believe suffering will end." I returned the pamphlet, thanked her, and closed the door." I was pressed for time. I was borderline rude.

I might have answered "yes" to her question at one time, that human suffering will end one day, but how could I answer in the affirmative now, less than three weeks after the unthinkable loss of life of defenseless Israelis at the hands of Hamas terrorists. Carnage was the predominant image in my mind when I answered "no" as to whether human suffering will ever end – not only the death of innocent Israelis but also Palestinians.

The two individuals at my front door were Jehovah's Witnesses. There is no doubt they would beg to differ with me. Jehovah's Witnesses believe the end of suffering is at hand, and God has promised to do away with all causes of human suffering, including crime, warfare, sickness, and natural disasters. I wasn't in the mood to debate them, although had I been, I might have chosen to debate "sickness" rather than "warfare." Each is equally deserving as a discussion point, but I'm a healer and not a politician.

I wanted to tell my impromptu guests that as a physician, I am committed to alleviating human suffering to the best of my ability through medical science and compassionate care. However, it is important to understand that suffering, in its various forms, is a part of the human condition. It is influenced by a multitude of factors beyond physical health, including psychological, social, environmental, and existential factors. Thus, while medical advancements continue to improve our ability to treat and prevent diseases, reducing physical suffering is beyond the scope of medicine to completely eliminate all forms of human suffering.

However, this doesn't mean we should stop striving to alleviate suffering wherever we can. As physicians, we are tasked with not only treating illness but also improving quality of life, providing comfort, and offering psychological and emotional support. These efforts, both big and small, contribute to reducing suffering in the world.

It's also been said that suffering can sometimes lead to personal growth and resilience. Many philosophical and spiritual traditions argue that suffering is a necessary part of life and can lead to greater wisdom and empathy. As a psychiatrist, I don't fully agree with that reasoning, especially as someone who has suffered in the past from serious depression. I would not wish it upon anyone.

Sir Winston Churchill was plagued throughout his life from recurrent episodes of severe depression, which he ruefully characterized as his "black dog," a faithful companion, sometimes out of sight, but always returning.

According to the *Oxford English Dictionary*, the first use of the phrase "black dog" to describe melancholy and depression was in 1776 by Samuel Johnson (refer to essay 22), the creator of the first English dictionary, who experienced episodes of depression throughout his life, particularly towards the end. Johnson called his melancholia "the black dog" in conversations and correspondence with his friends. Andrew Solomon, in *The Noonday Demon: An Anatomy of Depression*, states that both Abraham Lincoln and Winston Churchill "suffered from depression [and used] their anxiety and their concern as the basis for their leadership."

I find it difficult to believe that severely depressed persons can be effective leaders given that major depression results in marked indecisiveness, apathy, complete loss of pleasure (anhedonia) and slowed down mental and physical activities to the point of paralysis (psychomotor retardation). All of these features hamper the ability to lead.

William Styron, author of *Sophie's Choice*, said: "The pain of severe depression is quite unimaginable to those who have not suffered it, and it kills in many instances because its anguish can no longer be borne." Styron's memoir, *Darkness Visible*, discusses his public fight with depression, and his advocacy has helped others who have struggled with mental illness. Unlike another book I have read, *The Secret Strength of Depression*, depression has no silver lining, in my opinion. We are not better for having survived it. In fact, we are more likely to experience it again.

The late *60 Minutes* host Mike Wallace was also very public about his battle with depression and attempted suicide (by overdose). He had difficulty eating, sleeping and concentrating, and even after revealing to a family physician that he was worried about his mental state, Wallace said the doctor told him, "You're a tough guy. You'll get through it." Wallace's wife Mary believed he was suffering from clinical depression, but the doctor reportedly told the couple, "Forget the word 'depression' because that'll be bad for your image."

Had Wallace been successful in completing suicide, what would his image have been then? His body would have been six feet underground, and his legacy would have been tarnished due to the stigma of depression and suicide. Fortunately, Wallace sought psychiatric treatment and regained his health through psychotherapy and antidepressant medication.

I've witnessed much suffering in my career – physical sickness and mental illness – let alone other types of suffering mentioned by the Jehovah's Witnesses. My lived experience as a physician would have been the basis of informing them that I believe it's unlikely that human suffering will ever completely cease. I might have added that perhaps people capable of reaching great spiritual heights tend to suffer less, using Viktor Frankl as an example of someone who believed that meaning, even in suffering, could lead to transcendence and inner peace. In contrast to great religious figures and philosophers like Friedrich Nietzsche who viewed suffering as an integral part of the process that leads to personal growth ("that which does not kill us makes us stronger"), a more compassionate approach might be to acknowledge the reality of pain while supporting those who suffer, arguing that conditions like depression, trauma, or severe hardship often lack any inherent "secret strength" and can be debilitating rather than transformative.

42.
What are the Qualities of Exceptional Physicians?

The traits that make doctors great appear to be universal and internally driven. They can even be found in neurodiverse individuals.

From my extensive reading, I identified 10 qualities that I believe are common to exceptional doctors. Many of these qualities are virtuous and overlap with the same qualities seen in physicians with autism spectrum disorder (ASD) and other neurodivergent disorders, e.g., ADHD, sensory processing disorders, and certain learning disorders including dyslexia. This is no surprise given that medicine selects for many autistic-like strengths, such as analytical thinking, strong focus and concentration, preference for routine structure, and high level of expertise in certain areas.

Although the term "exceptional" sometimes has a negative connotation when applied to individuals with ASD – implying that autistic doctors would not make good clinicians, supervisors and educators – this stereotype is unwarranted. Judge for yourself by reviewing the qualities deemed essential to the making of outstanding physicians. Many of these qualities are, in fact, found in neurodivergent individuals, who constitute approximately 20% of the population.

1. **Medical Competency**: This is the first and foremost quality. An exceptional doctor has a broad base of medical knowledge and is aware of the most up-to-date treatments and technologies. They should have strong technical skills to perform procedures or operations effectively.

2. **Communication Skills**: Doctors need to be excellent communicators, not only with their patients but also with their colleagues and other healthcare professionals. They should be able to explain complex medical issues in a way that patients and their families can understand.

3. **Empathy**: Exceptional doctors genuinely care about their patients' well-being. They are able to understand and relate to their patients' experiences and emotions, which helps to build trust and improve patient outcomes.

4. **Professionalism**: This includes respect for patients, their families, and healthcare colleagues. It also covers maintaining patient confidentiality, being punctual, and dressing appropriately.

5. **Problem-Solving Skills**: Medicine can be unpredictable, and doctors often face complex cases. Exceptional doctors have strong analytical thinking and problem-solving skills to make accurate diagnoses and decide the best course of treatment.

6. **Life-Long Learner**: Medicine is a field that is constantly evolving with new research, treatments, and technologies. Exceptional doctors are committed to continuous learning and staying updated in their field.

7. **Leadership**: Doctors often lead healthcare teams and need to coordinate with other healthcare professionals. They should have strong leadership skills to manage their teams effectively.

8. **Patience**: Dealing with patients, especially those who are seriously ill or in pain, requires a lot of patience. Doctors should be able to remain calm and composed even in stressful situations.

9. **Attention to Detail**: From diagnosing diseases to writing prescriptions, doctors need to be meticulous to ensure that they do not miss anything.

10. **Resilience**: The medical profession can be physically and emotionally demanding. Exceptional doctors have the resilience to cope with long

hours, high-stress situations, and dealing with sickness and death.

Asking medical residents their opinions about the characteristics that distinguish truly outstanding doctors provides unique insights. Internal medicine specialist Ami L. DeWaters, MD, MSc, and colleagues conducted a survey of residents at 10 training institutions. The residents were asked to nominate core faculty members whom they perceived as exceptional "system citizens," in other words, those having the critical thinking skills and mindset to contribute to the holistic needs of individual patients, populations of patients, and the health system to achieve the best outcomes.

Eleven physicians from 289 nominations were selected as standouts and interviewed. Eight characteristics of an exceptional systems citizen were identified. These physicians:

- Are generous, selfless, humble, adaptable and resolute.
- Express values that drive behaviors "above and beyond" their colleagues' expectations.
- Are intentional about – and experts at – teaming.
- Are calm in the "eye of the storm."
- Employ a wide array of creative systems thinking skills to solve problems.
- Have exemplary interpersonal and communication skills.
- Teach systems-based practice as part of clinical care.
- Identify personal and professional mentors as key to their development.

It seems that no matter how you measure "exceptional," individuals have internal drivers that push them towards being great physicians. Intrinsic motivation plays a significant role in shaping an exceptional physician. This includes a strong desire to help others, a deep interest in the science of medicine, and a commitment to lifelong learning. These internal drivers not only motivate physicians to excel in their work but also help them to navigate the challenges and stresses of the medical profession.

Neurologist and physician life coach Sofia Dobrin, MD, believes that the definition of greatness ultimately should be tied to personal goals and self-worth. By redefining greatness to inner-focused criteria, ones that physicians can control, success seems to come more naturally and is less dependent on forces beyond their control.

For example, greatness could mean:

- I treat each patient with dignity and respect.
- I focus all my attention on the person in front of me and try to minimize distractions.
- I try to understand their condition the best I can.
- I look up what I don't know or don't understand or ask someone who does.
- I find out what is the best method of communication for my patient and communicate in that way.
- I remain curious and compassionate throughout my encounters.
- I allow them to ask questions.
- I remain open and curious rather than closed off.

Outstanding physicians, regardless of how they are defined, are easily recognizable. They are the ones who go the extra mile for their patients, who are always up-to-date with the latest medical advancements, who handle stressful situations with grace, and who inspire others with their dedication and passion for medicine. Their exceptional qualities not only benefit their patients but also contribute to the overall quality of healthcare. They set a high bar for medical practice and serve as role models for other physicians.

43.
Practicing Medicine with Conviction

Recognizing and utilize resources and opportunities that are already present within your immediate environment.

What does it take for physicians to practice with conviction – to practice medicine with a sense of confidence and commitment, passionate about your work? What factors allow medical students to enter the resident pool each July and turn their timidness into poise? How do you learn to stand by your medical convictions and base your decisions on a deep understanding of the patient combined with the latest evidence-based practices? Here are a few thoughts that come to mind.

First and foremost is continuous learning. You can practice with conviction by being well-informed and up-to-date about the latest medical advancements, research, and practices. This includes attending medical conferences, participating in professional development activities, and reading the latest medical journals.

I suggest you read (or skim) at least one major medical journal each week, like *The New England Journal of Medicine* or the *Journal of the American Medical Association* (*JAMA*), and two highly regarded journals in your specialty. A daily or weekly online newsfeed is also useful. Why not listen to a podcast on your way into work?

The pace of medical advancements can sometimes be overwhelming, making it challenging for you to stay updated. You must find the time to read, however, because reading bolsters your confidence and strengthens your commitment. The more knowledge and experience you have, the more conviction you will have in your decisions and actions. This comes from years of practice, dealing with various cases, and learning from successes and failures – and you will fail, make no mistake about it. The Institute of Medicine wrote *To Err is Human*. I keep a placard in my office that reads: "I am willing to make mistakes if someone else is willing to learn from them."

Doctors with conviction are able to empathize with their patients. They understand their concerns, fears, and expectations, which helps them provide the best possible care. We must never let our empathy wane. When choosing a physician, patients value affective concern as much as, if not more than, technical competence. I am dismayed by studies showing empathy decreasing midway through medical school, before students even add "MD" or "DO" after their names. Medical students should realize that physicians who are more attuned to the psychosocial needs of their patients are more likely to have better outcomes.

A physician practicing with conviction adheres strictly to medical ethics. This includes respecting patients' rights, maintaining confidentiality, and avoiding any form of discrimination. We are at a tipping point where the promulgation of diversity, equity and inclusiveness initiatives are beginning to eradicate barriers to treatment for minority populations while promoting a more diverse physician workforce. Diversity – or the lack of it – among medical students and physicians affects not only how care is delivered but also the ability to make clinical decisions with conviction and courage.

A nurturing environment is essential to practicing with conviction. Trainees are more capable of rising to a clinical challenge when they are respected and treated well. Our collective experience reveals that it is not a health system or long working hours that guarantees residents become excellent physicians; it's the conviction and dedication of the people within those systems and who schedule the hours.

In order to practice with conviction, certain barriers must be overcome.

The most important is imposter syndrome (IS), as I discussed in essay 40. People often think of imposter syndrome as a lack of self-confidence, and although that is certainly a feature, the hallmark of IS is an internal feeling of intellectual phoniness, a persistent belief that you are really not bright and have fooled anyone who thinks otherwise. Individuals with IS are high achievers, but they doubt their accomplishments and believe they are unwarranted.

Anyone who dreads being exposed as a "fraud" cannot practice with confidence. You will be saddled with doubts and fears of failing, as well as constant anxiety. Physicians with IS may be less likely to seek help or advice from their colleagues due to fear of appearing incompetent. This can hinder communication and teamwork, which are crucial in the management of patients.

A lack of confidence can also be perceived by patients, potentially undermining their trust in doctors and the profession. The first time I was called on to perform venipuncture I was a nervous wreck. My hands were trembling. My forehead was sweating. The patient was keenly aware of my insecurity and refused to allow me to draw blood. My confidence was shaken, and I shied away from performing procedures afterward.

Burnout also affects doctors' commitment and passion for their work. A major cause of burnout is chronic stress often brought on by practicing with limited resources, whether it's time, staff, equipment, or funding, which can prevent physicians from providing the best care possible, affecting their conviction. Physicians can take action to prevent burnout and seek help early when it occurs, restoring their commitment to practice.

Clinical uncertainties and treatment ambiguities can sometimes affect a physician's conviction, especially in the context of malpractice litigation. Simply the fear of litigation can make physicians practice defensive medicine rather than making decisions based solely on their professional judgment. The manner in which doctors deal with uncertainty affects their emotional well-being and ultimately their conviction to practice. Your interest in and commitment to practice will skyrocket once you learn that medicine is not always black and white and you develop skills to better tolerate ambiguity (refer to essay 32).

Systemic pressures – pressures from insurance companies, hospital administrators, and many other parties tied to the "medical-industrial complex" – can sometimes force doctors to make decisions that they are not entirely comfortable with, thereby affecting their conviction. Moral injury resulting from the failure of health systems to protect physicians during and after COVID has made them rethink their commitment to medicine, and they are leaving practice in droves. Healthcare institutions should focus on administrative and climate interventions to prevent and address moral injury and secure the physician workforce.

Finally, institutions and academicians must look more carefully at their processes to make sure those creative, out-of-the-box thinkers with potential are not lost in the shuffle of medical school and early career practice.

A case in point is Katalin ("Kati") Karikó, a pioneering American-Hungarian biochemist and researcher. Karikó was rejected for a tenure track post at The University of Pennsylvania Perelman School of Medicine; she was told she was "not of faculty quality." Karikó was demoted and her pay was cut, so she left Penn and obtained a job in 2013 working for the German drugmaker BioNTech. Ten years later, Karikó and her colleague Drew Weissman, MD, PhD, won the Nobel Prize in Physiology or Medicine for their work on messenger-RNA research that paved the way for COVID-19 vaccines.

I highlight Karikó's story because it's inspirational in the same vein as Russell Conwell's (1843-1925) famous "Acres of Diamonds" speech, which became the impetus for the founding of Temple University, my alma mater for medical school and business school. The story tells of an African farmer who envied other farmers whose fields were rich with diamonds, not realizing his own farm contained diamonds in raw form. Each and every one of us is a diamond in the rough waiting to be cultivated. Educators should never forget their obligation to students and to help them realize their full potential, carefully identifying students who may waiver in conviction and doubt their own abilities, so that these students may be lifted up and allowed to sparkle as bright as a diamond.

44.
AI Overtakes Humans – Fantasy or Reality?

Are the AI safeguards currently in place sufficient to prevent a doomsday scenario?

Artificial intelligence (AI) is one of the most talked about and hyped developments in recent years. It has transformed operations across numerous sectors, from manufacturing to financial services. In the health sector, AI has ushered in groundbreaking advancements in several areas, including psychotherapy, substituting for therapists and also posing ominous portents for physicians. AI systems that learn independently and autonomously – as opposed to iteratively – are the ones to keep an eye on.

Iterative learning and autonomous learning differ in terms of process and decision-making scope. Iterative learning involves a step-by-step process where an AI model is trained through repeated cycles or iterations. Each cycle refines the model based on errors or feedback from the previous iteration. This type of learning often involves human supervision, with periodic interventions to adjust hyperparameters, refine datasets, or evaluate outcomes. In a healthcare setting, iterative AI might be used in diagnostic tools that analyze imaging data, where radiologists provide feedback on the AI's initial assessments, allowing the system to learn and improve its diagnostic accuracy.

In contrast, autonomous learning refers to an AI system's ability to independently acquire knowledge or adapt its behavior in real time without explicit instructions or frequent human input. These systems are self-guided, seeking and utilizing data or experiences on their own to enhance performance. They are adaptable to changing environments and can learn new tasks or optimize their performance in open-ended scenarios. Autonomous AI in health care could potentially manage routine tasks such as patient monitoring or medication management, making decisions based on clinical signs and symptoms. Robotic surgery systems can make real-time adjustments during procedures, utilizing AI to enhance precision and efficiency.

Both approaches are valuable and are often combined in practice. For instance, iterative learning might pre-train a model that subsequently engages in autonomous learning during deployment, fine-tuning its abilities based on real-world data. This combination allows for both structured development and dynamic adaptability.

A compelling example where both iterative and autonomous AI approaches are combined in health care is in the development and deployment of personalized medicine platforms, particularly in oncology, where iterative AI is initially used to train models on large datasets comprising genetic information, treatment outcomes, and patient histories, and autonomous AI analyzes new patient data, recommending personalized treatment plans based on the insights derived from its extensive pre-training.

If you watch a lot of science fiction, like I do, then perhaps the fear of autonomous AI systems "taking over" and eliminating human functions – or humans themselves – feels both familiar and unsettling. It is a topic fueled not only by science fiction and fantasy but also philosophical debate. Former Google chairman and CEO Eric Schmidt's new book *Genesis: Artificial Intelligence, Hope, and the Human Spirit* has been described as "[a] profound exploration of how we can protect human dignity and values in an era of autonomous machines." I'm worried about protecting our species – let alone our "spirit."

Theoretically, several factors currently prevent doomsday scenarios. These can be divided into technical limitations, ethical safeguards, social structures, and systemic dependencies.

Technical Limitations

Autonomous AI systems are highly specialized and lack general intelligence. While they excel in narrow tasks, they do not possess the creative, emotional, or abstract thinking capabilities required for broad, human-like cognition. Current AI systems operate within strict parameters, and their decision-making is bound by the data and algorithms they are trained on. Even advanced systems that can adapt or learn in real-time are limited in scope and do not have the capacity for complex, independent planning or motivation – essential components for "taking over."

Ethical Safeguards

AI development is guided by ethical principles, regulations, and oversight designed to prevent harm. Developers and governments are implementing frameworks such as AI ethics guidelines, explainability requirements, and safety measures to ensure AI systems act in accordance with human values. Examples include the European Union's AI Act and AI ethical principles recommended by the U.S. Department of Defense and organizations like OpenAI (there are 200 or more guidelines and recommendations for AI governance worldwide). These guardrails aim to prevent misuse or unintended consequences.

Social Structures

AI systems are tools created, owned, and operated by humans or organizations. They lack autonomy in the sense of independence from these structures. Governments, institutions, and corporations establish rules and maintain oversight over how AI is deployed, ensuring that it serves specific purposes and remains under human control. Social and political systems also resist relinquishing significant power to autonomous systems due to economic, ethical, and existential concerns.

Systemic Dependencies

Autonomous AI systems depend on infrastructure, energy, and maintenance, all of which remain under human control. They cannot sustain themselves without these resources. Furthermore, AI systems often require human input or oversight for ongoing relevance and adaptation, particularly in unpredictable environments.

Preventing Harm

The idea of AI systems intentionally "eliminating" humans assumes a level of sentience, malice, and motive that current AI lacks. AI systems do not have desires, self-preservation instincts, or moral reasoning. Any harm caused by AI arises from flawed design, inadequate safeguards, or malicious use by humans – not from the systems themselves. Efforts to mitigate such risks focus on robust design, testing, and mandating accountability in AI deployment.

Future Considerations

As AI evolves, ensuring its alignment with human values and control becomes increasingly critical. This includes developing general AI, also known as Artificial General Intelligence (AGI), a type of AI that possesses the ability to understand, learn, and apply knowledge across a wide range of tasks at a level comparable to human intelligence. The development of AGI is a major goal in the field of AI research, but it remains largely theoretical at this point, as current AI systems are specialized and lack the generalization capabilities of human cognition.

Public discourse, interdisciplinary collaboration, and regulatory oversight will play pivotal roles in preventing scenarios where AI could displace humans in destructive ways. While theoretical risks exist, the current state of AI lacks the capacity or motive for such dramatic outcomes. Vigilance in research, ethical frameworks, and societal control will continue to guarantee that AI systems augment human capabilities rather than threaten them.

To Boldly Go

If you are not convinced of that future reality, I suggest you watch the original Star Trek episode "The Ultimate Computer." An advanced artificially intelligent control system, the M-5 Multitronic unit, malfunctions and engages in real war rather than simulated war, putting the Enterprise and a skeleton crew at risk. Kirk disables M-5, but he must gamble on the humanity of an opposing starship captain to not retaliate against the Enterprise. The Enterprise is spared. Kirk tells Mr. Spock that he knew the captain personally, "I knew he would not fire. An advantage of man versus machine."

God help us should we lose that advantage.

45.
Political Discussions in the Doctor-Patient Relationship

Political discussions can be polarizing and may inadvertently cause emotional or psychological distress to patients.

I don't recall politics being so contentious and front-and-center as it was during the 2024 Presidential election. Considering the sharp political divides across the U.S. and the omnipresence of social media, I suppose it was expected.

However, what I never anticipated was finding a note in a patient's chart by a healthcare provider stating, "We again discussed … the importance of voting and the safety, security, and effectiveness of voting by mail." It seems to me that there is already too much medical information to cover during a 10 to 15-minute primary care visit to include discussions about politics.

Nevertheless, politics – identity politics in particular – has found a medical voice, underscoring the importance of striving for a healthcare system that is inclusive, equitable, and responsive to the realities of all patients. There is a presumption that doctors should be as concerned with politics as they are with medicine.

"Identity politics" refers to political positions and perspectives that are based on the interests and viewpoints of social groups with which people identify. These groups can be defined by various characteristics such as race, gender, sexuality, religion, or other markers of identity. The core idea is that individuals from these groups advocate for policies and social changes that address their specific needs and experiences, often in response to historical and systemic inequities.

In recent years, identity politics has increasingly infiltrated the medical field. This trend can be seen in several ways. First, medical education and training programs are placing greater emphasis on cultural competence and sensitivity to diversity. This includes understanding how social determinants of health, such as race and socioeconomic status, impact patient outcomes.

Second, there is a growing recognition within the healthcare community of the need to address implicit bias and health disparities and inequities. Professional organizations and advocacy groups are pushing for policies that aim to reduce these disparities, such as expanding access to healthcare for marginalized groups: racial and ethnic minorities, LGBTQ+ community, people living in poverty, disabled individuals, and immigrants and refugees.

Third, physicians are becoming more aware of the importance of considering a patient's identity in their care. This can mean being sensitive to how a patient's background might affect their health and their interactions with the healthcare system. It also involves creating an inclusive and welcoming environment for all patients, regardless of their identity and gender.

Fourth, there is an increasing focus on collecting and analyzing data related to health outcomes across different identity groups. The FDA strongly encourages diversity action plans to increase clinical study enrollment of participants of historically underrepresented populations to help improve the data the agency receives about the patients who may potentially use medication and medical products. Public health initiatives are also becoming more tailored to address the specific needs of different identity groups. This targeted approach aims to improve health outcomes by identifying and addressing health disparities and considering the unique challenges and barriers faced by these groups.

While the incorporation of identity politics into the medical field aims to create a more equitable healthcare system, it also brings challenges.

These include navigating potential conflicts between different identity groups, balancing individual patient needs with broader social goals, and ensuring that efforts to address disparities do not inadvertently stigmatize or marginalize certain populations.

The question of whether doctors should discuss politics with their patients invites strong opinions on both the "left" and "right" sides. Liberals and conservatives essentially make the same arguments, i.e., physicians must protect patients from radical, divisive ideology, while arguing from extreme and opposite viewpoints.

Professional boundaries are a key consideration in this issue. The primary role of a physician is to provide medical care and support to their patients. Discussions should generally center around the patient's health, treatment options, and well-being. Introducing political discussions could potentially alienate or distress patients, which might damage the trust and rapport that are essential for an effective doctor-patient relationship.

Ethical considerations also play a significant role. Physicians should avoid causing harm, adhering to the principle of non-maleficence. Political discussions can be polarizing and may inadvertently cause emotional or psychological distress to patients. Additionally, respecting a patient's autonomy involves acknowledging their right to their own beliefs and values, which includes political views.

The situational context may sometimes necessitate political discussions, particularly when political issues directly impact patient health, such as policies on healthcare access, reproductive rights, and gender identity. In such cases, it might be appropriate to discuss these topics in a way that is informative and specific to the patient's care. If a patient initiates a political discussion and it is relevant to their concerns or care, a physician could engage, but should do so carefully, ensuring the discussion remains respectful and professional.

Practically, physicians might find it best to maintain a neutral stance if political topics arise, focusing on how policies may affect health and well-being rather than expressing personal political opinions. If a political discussion starts to become contentious, it may be helpful to gently steer the conversation back to the patient's health and care.

While there may be instances where discussing political matters is relevant and necessary, it should be approached with caution, always prioritizing the patient's health, comfort, and the integrity of the doctor-patient relationship.

46.
How Will You Make Your Mark on Medicine?

Whether in academia or private practice, find a way to leave your footprint.

Just as a carbon footprint measures the impact of human activities on the environment, the concept of an "academic footprint" can be used to describe the impact a physician makes in their field throughout their career.

The "academic footprint" of a physician includes the knowledge they impart, the research they conduct, the papers they publish, and the innovations they introduce. It represents their contribution to the advancement of medical science and the betterment of patient care. This footprint is not just important – it is essential – and can be made within and outside the halls of academia.

Physicians should aim to increase their academic footprint to enrich the medical field. The larger the academic footprint, the greater the influence and impact a physician has on the evolution of healthcare. The breadth and depth of this footprint can shape treatment protocols, influence healthcare policies, and inspire the next generation of physicians.

However, some physicians have a limited academic footprint. In the case of hospitalists, for example, one study found that among 1,554 academic hospital medicine faculty from 25 academic medical centers, only 42 (2.7%) were full professors and 140 (9%) were associate professors. The number of publications per academic hospital medicine faculty was noticeably low, with a mean of 6.3, and more than half (51%) had no published papers. Promotion was uncommon in academic hospital medicine, which may be partially due to low rates of scholarly productivity.

Measuring the Size of a Footprint

The findings suggest that measuring a physician's academic footprint involves a variety of factors that reflect their contributions to medical science and education. One key metric is their published research, including the number of papers they've authored, the quality of the journals these papers have been published in, and the number of citations these papers receive from other researchers. This offers an indication of their contribution to advancing medical knowledge.

Altmetrics – various "alternative" indicators of how influential published works become – are widely used in medicine and other scholarly pursuits. Yet, these indicators are not without controversy. Nevertheless, statistics on the number of downloads/citations of papers and the prestige/competitiveness of journals and journal articles are frequently used to evaluate academic footprints.

Another important metric is physicians' involvement in teaching and mentorship. This includes the number of students they've instructed, the number of physicians they've mentored, and the feedback they've received in these roles.

Physicians' impact on clinical guidelines and policy can also be considered. This could be measured by their involvement in professional bodies, task forces, or committees that shape healthcare policies and clinical practices.

Innovation in patient care, such as the development of new treatment protocols or the introduction of novel technologies in a physician's practice, can also be a part of their academic footprint.

Doctors routinely make other invaluable contributions beyond clinical care and medical education (e.g., in areas of governance, medical leadership, quality improvement, and social justice advocacy). Also, physicians are increasingly disseminating their contributions via newer mediums such as social media and podcasts that arguably have a greater reach than traditional scholarship outlets. People trust their opinions, and thus their endorsements carry a considerable amount of weight.

Motivating Trainees to Leave Their "Mark"

It is important for physicians to motivate medical students and residents to leave their "mark" on medicine. Physicians can motivate trainees by leading through example, showing them the impact of leaving an academic footprint in medicine – for example, by initiating the sequential steps in the adage "see one, do one, teach one."

Physicians should emphasize the benefits of an academic footprint, such as professional growth, recognition in the medical community, and the satisfaction of advancing medicine. They can also highlight that this footprint can lead to opportunities for collaboration, influence in shaping healthcare policies, and the ability to make a difference in patient care on a larger scale.

Mentorship is another effective way for physicians to motivate students and residents. Through one-on-one mentoring, physicians can guide them in their academic pursuits, provide feedback and support, and help them navigate the challenges of medical research and education.

Lastly, physicians can foster a culture of lifelong learning and curiosity. Encouraging students and residents to ask questions, seek answers, and continually expand their knowledge will naturally lead to a greater academic footprint. This can be facilitated by creating an environment that values and rewards academic contributions, innovation, and critical thinking.

Non-Academic Settings

It should be noted that while practicing in an academic medical center can facilitate academic contributions, it is not a prerequisite for leaving an academic footprint. Activities pursued outside of academic settings can also leave a lasting imprint. Physicians in private practice, for example, can conduct clinical research, contribute to medical literature, and participate in professional organizations that influence healthcare policy. They can also mentor medical students or residents in their offices or through affiliations with medical schools. An "adjunct" appointment at my medical school alma mater has enabled me to extend my academic footprint for the past two decades.

Physicians who focus on "doctoring" are still contributing to the medical field. They are applying the latest research findings to patient care, they are often involved in the education of patients and their families, and they are contributing to the collective knowledge of patient care.

Whether a doctor chooses to be involved in academia or to focus solely on clinical practice, their work is valuable and necessary. Either way, leaving a significant footprint should be a goal for every physician, just as reducing our carbon footprint is a collective responsibility. Both are about making a positive difference – in the world and in the field of medicine.

47.
The Dual Role of Illusion in Patient Care

From painted leaves to placebo, we must balance hope and honesty.

"The Last Leaf" by O. Henry, published in 1907 in his collection *The Trimmed Lamp and Other Stories of the Four Million*, follows the story of "Johnsy" (Joanna), a young, impoverished artist who is seriously ill with pneumonia. Feeling hopeless, she believes she will die once the last leaf falls from the vine outside her window. Johnsy's downstairs neighbor, Behrman, an aging artist considered a "failure in art," creates an illusion to inspire her by painting a leaf on the wall, which helps restore Johnsy's will to live. Ironically, though Johnsy recovers, Behrman – who braved the frigid damp night to paint the leaf – catches pneumonia and dies. The story powerfully underscores the role of illusion in medicine, illustrating how it can deeply influence patient care, for better or worse.

Beneficial Uses of Illusion in Medicine

1. **Placebo Effect**: One of the clearest examples of a beneficial illusion in medicine is the placebo effect. When patients believe they are receiving effective treatment, even if it's an inactive substance, they can experience real symptom relief. This highlights how a patient's perception can lead to tangible physical and psychological improvements. Studies suggest that the placebo effect can alleviate pain, reduce anxiety, and even improve outcomes in various chronic conditions. This reflects how belief, or the "illusion" of treatment, can mobilize the body's own resources for healing.

2. **Therapeutic Communication**: Physicians may also use illusion in communication, intentionally framing their words and actions to instill confidence and reassurance. For example, a physician may project calm and certainty in a serious diagnosis or downplay possible adverse effects to avoid overwhelming a patient with anxiety. This illusion of control and reassurance can help patients feel safer and less fearful, which can have positive effects on their overall treatment experience and may even enhance their recovery.

3. **Environmental Illusions**: In some healthcare settings, environments are designed to create comforting illusions. For instance, many hospitals use nature-inspired art, soothing lighting, and even virtual reality experiences to reduce patient stress and improve comfort. This illusion of being in a serene, non-clinical space can lower blood pressure and stress hormone levels, which are important for healing and recovery, particularly in high-stress environments like intensive care units.

4. **Cognitive Behavioral Therapy (CBT)**: While not an illusion in the traditional sense, CBT involves changing the way patients perceive and interpret their thoughts and experiences, allowing them to gain control over their reactions and break free from self-defeating patterns of behavior. By altering these perceptions, patients can reduce symptoms of depression and anxiety, effectively changing their mental states.

5. **Hypnosis**: During hypnosis, patients enter a deeply relaxed state and may experience changes in sensation, perception, and memory, which can be seen as a form of illusion. This altered state allows them to explore thoughts and feelings in a way that can lead to therapeutic benefits. For instance, hypnosis can aid in managing chronic pain by altering the patient's perception of it, creating a situation that lessens the pain's intensity. I experienced this firsthand years ago after sustaining a painful football injury. Just the anticipation of the emergency physician's examination intensified

my pain. With my consent, he hypnotized me, allowing him to manipulate my neck and shoulder to diagnose a broken collarbone, later confirmed by X-ray.

Detrimental Effects of Illusion in Medicine

1. **Placebo Effect**: The placebo effect acts as a double-edged sword: while it shows the powerful influence of mind on body and offers insights into non-medication-based healing mechanisms, it also complicates the clinical landscape, making it harder to assess true treatment efficacy and adding ethical layers to patient care and clinical trials. Psychiatric patients, especially those with conditions like depression and anxiety, tend to respond more favorably to placebos than patients with purely physiological illnesses. This robust placebo response can make it difficult to accurately measure the efficacy of psychiatric medications.

2. **False Reassurance and Misdiagnosis**: Sometimes, illusions can mislead both the patient and the clinician. Overly optimistic language or reassurance, if misused, may give patients a false sense of security. If a physician downplays symptoms or glosses over risks, patients might ignore early signs of complications or delay seeking necessary care. This illusion can ultimately delay proper diagnosis and treatment, leading to worse outcomes.

3. **The Illusion of Certainty**: In some cases, clinicians present diagnoses or prognoses with a degree of certainty that is not warranted, creating an illusion of absolute knowledge where ambiguity actually exists. This is particularly problematic in complex or poorly understood conditions, where the physician's confidence might prevent patients from seeking second opinions or alternative therapies. Such certainty can also hinder shared decision-making, making patients feel less empowered to ask questions or express concerns.

4. **Overuse of Diagnostic Technology**: The illusion created by high-tech diagnostic tools can also mislead both patients and physicians. Advanced imaging and lab tests often produce detailed information that may not be clinically relevant, but they can create an illusion of "seeing something." This can lead to overdiagnosis, where minor anomalies are treated as serious issues, or to an overreliance on tests rather than a holistic assessment of the patient. Both scenarios can cause unnecessary anxiety, lead to invasive procedures, or even cause harm from overtreatment.

A Delicate Balance

Just as Behrman's painted leaf offers Johnsy the hope she needs to survive, illusions in medicine can inspire optimism and even trigger real physiological benefits. Yet, illusions also carry risks when they distort reality, leading to overconfidence, misdiagnosis, or lost opportunities for meaningful patient engagement. The story of "The Last Leaf" reminds us of the delicate balance in medicine between using illusions to foster hope and ensuring they do not mislead, as they hold both promise and responsibility within patient care. Clinicians must use this power wisely within the ethical framework of medical practice.

48.
The Decline of Whole-Person Treatment in Modern Medicine

The principles of biopsychosocial treatment were articulated nearly 50 years ago, yet modern medicine seems to have left them behind.

A nurse practitioner responded to one of my op-eds in which I discussed the importance of reciprocity in the doctor-patient relationship. The nurse said:

"I feel so frustrated by the time constraints forced on us by using a business model of practice. In the 30-plus years I've been a nurse, we have moved from patient-centered care (which is the current inaccurate buzzword for the type of care we provide) to income-generated care. How many patients can we shove into an hour to bill insurance to maximize our bottom line? I'm looking at retiring early because I feel I can no longer give the quality nursing care I was trained to provide. I'm now told I don't work hard enough or fast enough to move people through. We no longer have the benefit of learning about and with our patients to provide care of the whole person. When I started nursing many years ago, the aspect that was drilled into us nursing students was dealing with the physiological and psychosocial aspect of the patient. For a patient to heal, the entire person needed to be addressed not just one area."

I've heard this sentiment many times from physicians and advanced practice providers who appear to long for a time when the biopsychosocial model was in vogue. This model was first conceptualized by George Engel, MD, in 1977, suggesting that to understand a person's medical condition it is not simply the biological factors that must be considered, but also the psychological and social factors. The value of Engel's heuristic approach to treatment became apparent when it was realized that social determinants of health account for approximately half of all health-related outcomes.

The following list was compiled by the World Health Organization and provides examples of the social determinants of health, which can influence health outcomes (and equity) in positive and negative ways:

- Income and social protection
- Education
- Unemployment and job insecurity
- Working life conditions
- Food insecurity
- Housing, basic amenities and the environment
- Early childhood development
- Social inclusion and non-discrimination
- Structural conflict
- Access to affordable health services of decent quality

It seems that the concept of whole-person treatment has waned since the turn of the century. We're more accustomed to practicing medicine in line with the biomedical model that dominated practice prior to Engel's seminal paper. I believe we are ignoring the psychological and social substrates of health care, and in doing so we fail to truly understand our patients' concerns, including their needs and desires. I wonder whether such neglect can partially explain the low rankings on key health indicators that have continued to fall as U.S. medical expenditures have skyrocketed, far outstripping those of healthier nations?

Grappling with psychosocial issues is far more complex and time-consuming than Engel ever imagined. But some of that is our own making. It's virtually impossible to assess non-biological dimensions of health when medical offices today are run like assembly lines and patient visits are held for 15 minutes. In Engel's era, most physicians were practicing independently and were spared productivity quotients. They were untethered to computer prompts and automated reminders. Fifty years ago, doctors made notations in their patients' charts to ask about important milestones – job promotions, graduations and anniversaries (marriage, sobriety, etc.). When was the last time your EMR system delivered this type of feedback?

The introduction of EMRs has resulted in as much harm as good: computers may cause "alert fatigue," with negative clinical consequences. When important social history is entered electronically, it often remains static, quickly becoming outdated. To add insult to injury, about 50% of the medical record is copied and pasted, making it difficult to find and verify information in day-to-day clinical work. Duplicated text in EMRs, so-called "note bloat," also leads to wasted clinician time, medical error, and burnout.

Physicians practicing in the 1970s were free thinkers and private investigators, guided by a deep understanding of their patients' social habits and milieu. Histories often referred to patients by their occupation ("Mrs. Jones is a 53-year-old school teacher…") rather than by gender pronoun. From the perspective of the patient, access to physicians improved during the 1970s. On average, a patient in 1971 had to wait only 5.6 days for a primary care appointment, and the average visit lasted 22 minutes.

In December 2022, I was seen in the emergency department of my local hospital for treatment of what turned out to be symptoms of influenza A and lobar pneumonia. I was told to follow up with my PCP to ensure the pneumonia had resolved. The earliest appointment I could schedule through the patient portal was 16 days, despite indicating "sick visit" as opposed to "routine visit." A call to my PCP's office put me in touch with his medical assistant. The best she could do was add me to a waiting list.

My PCP is a very good doctor, although paraphrasing the late Senator

Lloyd Bentsen, "he's no Marcus Welby." And maybe that's the problem. I'm old school. I'm stuck in the 1970s – me, my music and my medical expectations. I attended medical school in the 1970s. The hit television show Marcus Welby, MD was spawned in the 1970s. Dr. Welby was a family medicine physician with a kind bedside manner who made house calls and was personally involved with all his patients and their extended family members and support systems, or at least he made it his business to become involved. Welby was so devoted to his patients you would have sworn he had a caseload of one per day.

When the television series ended in 1976, Robert Young, the iconic actor who played Marcus Welby, quipped, "I knew that it was time to quit when I started taking time off to play golf!" His tongue-in-cheek remark portended a prime concern shared by modern-day physicians about their specialties – which one affords the greatest work-life balance? However, work ethic was never questioned in medical dramas that aired a half-century ago – not only Marcus Welby, MD, but also Ben Casey and Medical Center. While the new breed of medical TV shows, beginning with St. Elsewhere in 1982, portrayed gritty, realistic medical scenarios, they were better known for their ensemble casts and overlapping serialized storylines focusing more on the lives of doctors than the plight of patients.

I guess I'm just a hopeless traditionalist and unable to reconcile the demise of the biopsychosocial model and the physicians – fictional or not – who embodied its principles. Sure, I can pay a hefty yearly fee for concierge medicine and maybe enjoy a less rushed, more personalized experience with someone who knows and understands me better than my current PCP.

Yet, with or without time and productivity constraints imposed by health systems on their employee physicians, most doctors appear to be stuck in the purely biomedical model Engel sought to transform. My hope is that medical educators will re-instill in young trainees Engel's thesis that "the physician's basic professional knowledge and skills must span the social, psychological, and biological, for [their] decisions and actions on the patient's behalf involve all three."

49.
The Secret to Improving Healthcare Services

Use secret shoppers, including undercover doctors, to evaluate the quality of care in medical offices and hospitals.

Twice, an emergency-room nurse called out the name of a patient in the waiting room of a hospital. The patient did not respond, and the nurse had no idea he had already suffered a massive heart attack and was dead.

The nurse had never ventured beyond the waiting room doorway. She simply did not see the patient where he sat, unattended, for nearly an hour. Accounts given later by the nurse – that she had searched the waiting room for the patient – appeared to be refuted by surveillance video.

To make matters worse, thieves stole the patient's wristwatch as he sat unresponsive in the waiting room. The patient was a popular school guidance counselor and musician in the community.

A Novel Idea

About 4% of hospital deaths are due to preventable medical error, according to a 2019 meta-analysis published in *BMJ* (the figure is 6% across all types of medical care settings). Most errors are multifactorial and usually involve a failure of systems and services. It begs the question how to improve the delivery of healthcare services, not only in hospitals but in other medical settings such as doctor's offices, ambulatory centers, and urgent care and long-term facilities.

Surely there are many ways to tackle this challenge, but I would like to suggest a relatively untapped strategy for improving the effectiveness of medical services – specifically, the use of pseudo-patients. Also known as "secret shoppers" and "mystery shoppers," pseudo-patients are undercover consumers trained to feign illness or injury. They do so to evaluate how well the health system responds to their needs.

Many of us, especially those in the healthcare profession, make observations and impressions of the care we receive as patients. We make judgments about waiting room decor and office staff behavior before we ever see the doctor. After the appointment, don't we usually form an opinion about the doctor's bedside manner? Many of us record our encounters on one of several websites that profile and grade doctors' abilities based on our experiences with them.

In the retail industry, trained consumers have been providing feedback about the quality of customer service for years. However, using secret shoppers to gauge the effectiveness of medical services is a rather novel idea, even though the use of "pseudo-patients" dates back to the early 1970s when graduate students masqueraded as psychiatric patients and recorded their experiences in mental hospitals. This seminal study, conducted by the psychologist David Rosenhan and titled "On Being Sane in Insane Places," was published in *Science* and did much to undermine confidence in psychiatric services, in particular the validity and reliability of psychiatric diagnoses at the time.

How It Works

Secret shopping works like this: Physicians and healthcare administrators, unashamed to admit that their facilities may not be delivering top-notch quality services to patients, enlist the aid of a secret shopping company. These companies, in turn, hire and train consumers to evaluate medical services in the context of environmental ambience, staff demeanor and appearance, and business practices, to name a few.

To counter some of the ethical objections to secret shopping, all staff are informed up-front that secret shoppers will be passing through, although the time and location of their activities are not announced. Nor do secret shoppers make quality judgments about the actual care being rendered by physicians – only observations about how the doctors conducted themselves and whether, in the opinion of the secret shopper, the doctor adequately explained the reasons for ordering tests, procedures, and medication, including a discussion of possible side effects.

Despite efforts to make secret shopping transparent, many medical personnel resist participating in secret shopping programs because they view covert operations as deceitful under any condition. Objections have also been raised because secret shoppers may utilize medical resources unnecessarily and deprive or delay a real patient from getting needed care.

Most objections to secret shopping, however, can be tempered by the fact that, when facilities hire secret shoppers, they do so voluntarily, without coercion, in the name of quality improvement. The American Medical Association has noted that physicians have an ethical responsibility to engage in activities that contribute to continual improvements in patient care. Secret shopping is one such activity.

Medical Secret Shoppers

Medically trained secret shoppers, especially physicians, themselves, posing as patients, are virtually non-existent. However, they have the potential to probe deeply into the quality chasm. Physician secret shoppers could determine whether an examining physician made the correct diagnosis, or at least whether an appropriate differential diagnosis was formed. A skilled medical secret shopper could determine whether the examining physician's recommended therapy conformed to evidenced-based practice guidelines and whether appropriate consultation was considered, for example, in cases where physician secret shoppers portrayed complicated, difficult-to-diagnose patients.

Physicians sent incognito to make first-hand assessments about their colleagues' abilities would break new ground. They may not be popular with other physicians, but they will signal those outside the medical profession that physicians are vested in innovative quality improvement activities and seek to be the ultimate stewards of care.

The importance of physician ownership of the quality improvement process must be underscored. It is the primary reason I have worked in the health insurance industry. At this stage of my career, however, close to retirement, I was wondering whether other physicians like me – those considering retirement but not intent on becoming couch potatoes – would care to join me in an encore career and become a secret shopper?

50.
Disability Redefines "Ability" in the Medical Profession

Creativity and adaptability contribute to the success of doctors with disabilities.

Elton John has lost significant vision in both eyes due to an infection and is unsure whether he can record an album again. Paul Simon recently revealed that hearing loss has caused him to drop certain songs from his live performances. Simon remarked, "You know Matisse, when he was suffering at the end of his life, when he was in bed, he envisioned all these cut-outs and had a great creative period. So, I don't think creativity stops with disability. So far, I haven't experienced that. And I hope not to."

Henri Matisse's late-life work with gouache-painted paper cut into forms with scissors, known as *gouaches découpées*, is a testament to how creativity can adapt and even flourish in the face of physical limitations. Confined to a wheelchair after surgery for abdominal cancer in 1941, Matisse turned exclusively to this vibrant, innovative art form and created masterpieces like *The Snail, Memory of Oceania, and Blue Nude II*. His cut-outs reflect not only his artistic genius but also his resilience and ability to reimagine his medium when traditional painting became impossible. This period, often considered one of his most iconic, underscores the idea that physical disability doesn't hinder creativity – it can even open new pathways for expression.

Reading about Matisse got me thinking about disability as it relates to doctors. Disability can significantly alter the careers of physicians, possibly forcing them into another specialty, profession, or retirement. It may or may not make them more creative – it depends on several factors, such as their specialty, type of disability, and resiliency.

Adapting Medical Practice

A physician's specialty often plays a major role in their ability to adapt. Surgical and procedural fields, for instance, require fine motor skills, physical stamina, and precision, meaning disabilities affecting these functions may prompt shifts toward less physically demanding roles such as teaching, research, or administrative work. Conversely, specialties like psychiatry, pathology, and radiology often allow greater flexibility for physicians with physical or mobility challenges.

The type of disability clearly determines the level of adaptation required. Physicians with physical disabilities may rely on assistive technologies, such as adapted surgical instruments or voice-activated software, to maintain their practice. Those with sensory impairments, such as blindness or deafness, have successfully practiced medicine by leveraging accommodations like interpreters, Braille, or tactile medical devices.

My medical school alma mater, Temple University, made national news in 1972 when they accepted a blind student: David W. Hartman. Sightless since age 8, Hartman had been rejected by 10 other schools despite graduating Gettysburg College Phi Beta Kappa with a 3.8 grade point average. Hartman went on to a successful career in psychiatry, choosing that field because he "love[d] to hear people's story," while also noting that blindness was a minor impairment in medical school given that about 85% of diagnosis consists of a good history, and most of the physical is based upon touch, listening, and even smell.

Robert H. Babcock is another example of a blind physician. Babcock managed cadaver dissection by touch and later wrote acclaimed books on diseases of the heart and the lungs, eventually becoming president of the Society of Internal Medicine of Chicago.

Mental health conditions, while increasingly recognized and supported as disabilities, still carry stigma within the medical profession, potentially complicating efforts to seek help or accommodations. Systemic barriers can exacerbate these challenges. A culture that values the "invincible" physician often discourages acknowledgment of disability, fostering fears of being perceived as less competent. Licensing and credentialing processes can subject disabled physicians to additional scrutiny, particularly around perceived risks to patient safety. Workplace accommodations, while critical, vary widely in availability and effectiveness.

Innovative Tools

Disability may not inherently spark traditional creativity, but it often compels physicians to develop innovative adaptations. Some find new roles that make use of their expertise, such as teaching, mentoring, or contributing to public health and advocacy efforts. Experiencing disability firsthand can also enhance their empathy for patients, deepening their clinical practice. Problem-solving skills honed through personal adaptation may further enrich their professional contributions. Hartman, for example, worked with patients with disabilities after his residency and later subspecialized in addiction medicine.

Artificial intelligence (AI) (refer to essay 44) has also shown promise for assisting people with disabilities and might correct for the under-representation of individuals with disabilities trained as physicians. For example, AI-driven voice recognition software allows physicians with mobility impairments to dictate notes, navigate electronic health records, and communicate with patients without relying on manual inputs. AI-powered diagnostic tools, such as image analysis software, can reduce the physical and cognitive workload by providing rapid, accurate interpretations of radiological or pathological data. Additionally, adaptive technologies integrated with AI, such as robotic surgical systems or prosthetic devices, can extend physical capabilities, allowing disabled physicians to perform tasks that might otherwise be challenging or even impossible.

Toward Greater Inclusivity

Physicians with disabilities often serve as advocates and role models, challenging stereotypes and advancing inclusivity in medicine. Their presence in the field encourages system-wide changes, such as better accommodations and more inclusive medical education. In doing so, they help redefine what it means to be a capable physician, shifting the focus toward cognitive, emotional, and interpersonal competencies rather than physical ability alone. For example, many physiatry physicians with disabilities are known for their innovative approaches to rehabilitation medicine, empowering patients with disabilities to regain independence.

Although disability may alter a physician's career trajectory, it does not have to diminish their capacity to make meaningful contributions. In many cases, it opens unexpected avenues for impact, shaping and diversifying not only individual careers but also the broader culture of medicine. As technologies like AI continue to make the profession more accessible, these dynamics may further transform how we define and support diversity in medical practice.

Overcoming disability barriers to a career in medicine requires both creativity and adaptability. Preparing students with students for medical practice likewise demands creativity. In essence, it takes imagination, not sight, to be a good physician.

Afterword

The Graduation Speech I've Longed to Give

I've been blessed to be able to attend the "white coat" ceremonies of two of my children – one is a physician and the other is a physician assistant – and my son-in-law, an emergency medicine resident. There were no white coat ceremonies in my era.

White coat ceremonies proliferated around the turn of the century, a rite of passage emphasizing a first-year medical student's commitment to demonstrate scientific proficiency, act professionally, earn the trust of patients and provide compassionate care. The ceremonial cloaking of medical students in white coats, as opposed to the original black garb worn by physicians, symbolizes cleanliness and purity associated with the era of antisepsis ushered in by Joseph Lister in the late 19th century. The ceremony has expanded to other health-related fields in recent years.

Attending my children's white coat ceremonies started me thinking about what my advice would be to up-and-coming physicians. It's a speech I've longed to make, but one I've never been asked to give. The speakers at white-coat ceremonies are featured by invitation only, and I'm still waiting for mine! But that hasn't stopped me from imagining what I might say to graduating medical students.

My main message would be to recognize that the fates of patients are beyond their control, so they should not blame themselves for bad outcomes; they should support each other through difficult and trying times and seek help if they become emotionally overwhelmed. Unwell medical students, like unwell physicians in practice, tend to lose their professional ideals, provide suboptimal care to patients, and have less successful careers than their healthier counterparts.

I would ask medical schools to ensure professional counseling is available for the approximately 50% of students who will burn out in medical school, the 15% who will become depressed and especially the 5% to 10% who will contemplate suicide. Too many struggling students (and physicians) manage to stay under the radar, so I need to tell them there is no shame in admitting to feelings of hopelessness and seeking help for anxiety and depression. Any traumatic experience can have immediate and lasting psychological effects, and medical education is no exception.

After the suicide deaths of two novice doctors in New York City within days of each other in August 2014, at a time when many white coat ceremonies were occurring in medical schools across the United States, well-known physician and author Danielle Ofri, MD, PhD, pleaded to students that they do not succumb to the "tyranny of medicine."

She commented, "Medical students are asked to absorb an immense body of knowledge. Prima facie, this is a seemingly reasonable request of our doctors-to-be. But the number of facts is larger than any human being can realistically acquire, and is ever expanding. Yet we act as though this perfection of knowledge is a realistic possibility. No wonder nearly every student feels like an imposter during his or her training."

I would inform the audience that imposter syndrome is a psychological construct characterized by the persistent belief that one's success is undeserved rather than due to personal effort, skill and ability. Family and friends may think imposter syndrome is not applicable to their loved ones, but the fact is a survey of more than 3,000 physicians showed that nearly one in four doctors across the career spectrum reported feeling like an imposter. The study's findings also suggested that imposter syndrome can develop during medical school and residency and continue beyond training, and the greater the identification with an imposter the higher the prevalence of suicidal ideation.

It should not be lost upon anyone that physicians have the highest suicide rates of any professional groups. Approximately one physician per day dies by suicide in the U.S. Lorna Breen, MD, and several other physicians who practiced on the front-lines of the COVID pandemic were victims of suicide. The Doctor Lorna Breen Heroes' Foundation was established to honor her memory and to fight for the professional and emotional well-being of health workers.

When these now-energized medical students eventually become disillusioned and question why they chose medicine as a profession, I want to tell them to look forward to the "human moments" in practice – taking care of people in their most vulnerable states and becoming somewhat vulnerable in the process, but not so vulnerable that they would not ask for help, if needed. They should seek out other students and faculty whom they can trust and can be vulnerable with, meeting with them at regular intervals to discuss the ups and downs of medical school and practice. We must cultivate a professional environment that allows medical students as well as trainees and full-fledged physicians to better support each other and "come clean" about their mental health problems without fear of retribution.

I will remind the distinguished faculty attending the ceremony that not all medical students who graduate will remain in practice or even enter the practice of medicine. Some, like me, will lean toward industry and non-traditional medical careers. They need to be nurtured and feel welcomed at medical school. They are not traitors to the profession. Quite the opposite. Students enrolled in dual-degreed MD-(DO)/MBA programs (or MPH programs) will provide new healthcare perspectives. They will not abandon their professional ideals. A business curriculum integrated with a medical education at any point in one's career will produce talented leaders.

I want to inform everyone that physician leadership is critical to steer health care into the future. For physicians, in a world dominated by nonmedical administrators in hospitals and health insurance companies, medical leadership is essential for health care to continue moving toward higher quality, consistent safety and streamlined efficiency. Evidence suggests that organizations and patients benefit when physicians take on leadership roles. The best performing hospitals in the U.S. are led by physicians.

I realize that most students who receive their white coats will practice medicine in the traditional sense, either as primary care doctors or specialists. I want them to know that they can still be effective medical leaders as busy clinicians. In fact, medical leadership may best be rendered through what is known as "expert authority," wherein a physician's unique and extensive knowledge of diseases and therapeutics, and of human nature, serves as the basis of their authority and the platform of leading. Medical leaders succeed by communicating their vision to people and organizations that recognize their value – so-called "leading by example" – and every physician has the ability to lead.

Harvard Medical School professor and quality expert Donald M. Berwick, MD, remarked to the 2010 graduates of Yale Medical School: "Those who suffer need you to be something more than a doctor; they need you to be a healer. And to become a healer, you must do something even more difficult than putting your white coat on. You must take your white coat off."

Berwick's advice on the surface appears to run counter to the white coat being seen as a powerful symbol of the medical profession and a shift toward a new era emphasizing patient care in a clean and controlled environment. But removing the coat doesn't negate a doctor's commitment to treating patients fairly, with dignity, and displaying the values of trust, professionalism, and ethical responsibility. Although physicians often do heroic things, taking off the white coat reminds us we are humans and subject to normal human limitations. We sometimes forget we are human when we wear our white coats. Keep in mind, white coats bear no resemblance to Superman's cape – and humans don't fly!

By virtue of being accepted into medical school, each and every medical student has been deemed competent and worthy to serve the suffering. What matters most is that these young and diverse doctors remain passionate about improving the quality of care for patients. A doctor can do that as a practicing physician, hospital CEO, or industry insider. Paraphrasing the incomparable Randy Newman ("You've Got a Friend in Me"), it doesn't matter whether you wear a white coat, a business suit, or nothing at all. You can leave your hat on.

Notes and Sources

All essays in this book were previously posted online at one of several websites: KevinMD, MedPage Today, Doximity, and SoMeDocs. They underwent minor editing and updating and were cross-referenced during the book's production. References to medical research, scientific studies, and quotations were intentionally omitted in order to improve the continuity of reading. To access source information, readers can search the essays by their titles on the internet and click on hyperlinked text within each essay.

Essays 20, 28, 29, 30, 33, 34, 36, 37, 38, 39, 40, and 48 appeared in *Every Story Counts: Exploring Contemporary Practice Through Narrative Medicine*, copyright © 2023 American Association for Physician Leadership®, 800-562-8088, www.physicianleaders.org, reprinted with permission.

About the Author

Arthur L. Lazarus, MD, MBA, is a healthcare consultant, certified physician executive, and nationally recognized author, speaker, and champion of physician leadership and wellness. He has broad experience in clinical practice and the health insurance industry, having led programs at Cigna and Humana. At Humana, Lazarus was vice president and corporate medical director of behavioral health operations in Louisville, Kentucky, and subsequently a population health medical director in the state of Florida.

Lazarus has also held leadership positions in several pharmaceutical companies, including Pfizer and AstraZeneca, conducting clinical trials, and reviewing promotional material for medical accuracy and FDA compliance. He has published more than 400 articles and essays online and in scientific and professional journals and has written and edited over a dozen books, many related to the field of narrative medicine.

Born in Philadelphia, Pennsylvania, Lazarus attended Boston University, where he graduated with a bachelor's degree in psychology with Distinction. He received his medical degree with Honors from Temple University School of Medicine, followed by a psychiatric residency at Temple University Hospital, where he was chief resident. After residency, Lazarus joined the faculty of Temple University School of Medicine, where he currently serves as Adjunct Professor of Psychiatry. He also holds non-faculty appointments as Executive-in-Residence at Temple University Fox School of Business and Management, where he received his MBA degree, and Senior Fellow, Jefferson College of Population Health, Philadelphia, Pennsylvania.

Well known for his leadership and medical management skills, Lazarus is a sought-after presenter, mentor, teacher, and writer. He has shared his expertise and perspective at numerous local, national, and international meetings and seminars.

Lazarus is a past president of the American Association for Psychiatric Administration and Leadership, a former member of the board of directors of the American Association for Physician Leadership (AAPL), and a current member of the AAPL editorial review board. In 2010, the American Psychiatric Association honored Lazarus with the Administrative Psychiatry Award for his effectiveness as an administrator of major mental health programs and expanding the body of knowledge of management science in mental health services delivery systems.

Lazarus is among a select group of physicians in the United States who have been inducted into both the Alpha Omega Alpha medical honor society and the Beta Gamma Sigma honor society of collegiate schools of business.

Lazarus enjoys walking, biking, playing piano, and listening to music. He has been happily married to his wife, Cheryl, for over 40 years. They are the proud parents of four adult children and the grandparents of six young children.

www.ingramcontent.com/pod-product-compliance
Lightning Source LLC
Chambersburg PA
CBHW070620030426
42337CB00020B/3865